Open
to the
Unknown

Open
to the
Unknown

Dialogues in Delphi
Jean Klein

Edited by Emma Edwards

Third Millennium Publications
St. Peter Port • London • Santa Barbara

Library of Congress Catalog Card No.: 92-064317

ISBN No.: 1-877769-18-5

Cover Art by John Chase Lewis

Design and typography by Janet Andrews

Desktop Studio, San Anselmo, CA

Printed in the United States of America

First Printing: August 1992

Acknowledgments

I profoundly thank all those whose gifts made this publication possible. Also Giorgos Mavrogiannis who translated the original dialogues, Mary Dresser and Janet Andrews who prepared the text for printing, Stephan Bodian who proofread the final copy, and especially my friend and editor Emma Edwards who gave all her insight and intelligence to this book.

Jean Klein

Other Works By Jean Klein

In English:
Transmission of the Flame
I Am
The Ease of Being
Be Who You Are
Who Am I?

In French:
Sois ce que tu es
L'ultime Réalité
La Joie sans Objet
L'insondable Silence

In German:
Freude im Sein

In Dutch:
Gesprekken met Jean Klein

In Spanish:
La Escucha Creativa
La Mirada Inocente
La Sencillez del ser
La Alegria Sin Objeto

Translations also available in Italian, Greek and Hebrew

Journals Edited by Jean Klein:
Listening
Etre (France)
Essere (Italy)
Ser (Spain)

Videotapes:
The Current of Love (with Lilias Folan)
The Flame of Being (with Michael Toms)
Love and Marriage (with Paul & Evelyn Moschetta)

Preface

We have come here together to explore and understand self-knowledge, our real nature. This inquiry asks for an open mind, free from all knowing and expectation. When the mind is free from knowledge and anticipation it is open to the unknown, available to the all-possible. Let us be knowingly in this openness. It is felt as love.

Meeting in Delphi

Peaceful earth softly pulsating
like the voice of the Guru
Coming from silence.

In front, as if on a screen, words
like wings,
Beat in the room.

Don't try to hold them.

Travel in their music, a river of light
you follow to the source, there present
the ancient vibration, The Oracle, the "E.I.M.I."
Octaves of water in Kastalia,
forms float air-like.

What are you looking for?
It is here.

As in the morning the scent of roses beckons.
Bend down to the flower.
Stay in the moment that unites.
Forever the garden, forever the rhythm,
forever the olive tree.
Forever the Teacher who opens the window.

Greek original by Yannis Plahovris,
Delphi 1990

November 3, 1990, Morning

We have come together to find out what we mean by truth, or our real nature, globality. This inquiry calls for a certain quality of attention, an attention free from any expectation. It is really a state of not-knowing, where we are simply open. It should also be clear that what we are looking for, we already are. It is completely objectless. Truth cannot be known by the mind and requires a different kind of perceiving than the mind uses. It is not a functional perceiving which is in duality—"I perceive this"—but a being the perceiving, where there is only perceiving without any perceiver or thing perceived. In other words, where we *are* the perceiving.

All that can be obtained, perceived, thought, is an object, but we are the subject of all objects. So if we remain in a state of trying to achieve understanding, we will only find an object and not the objectless truth. This object may be a subtle state, but what we are fundamentally is not a state. In trying to obtain ourselves, we go away from ourselves. When this is understood, our mind is automatically brought to a stop where all the energy used in projecting and attaining is no longer directed, and we find ourselves in non-directionless openness, waiting without waiting. This is really the most profoundly relaxed state of the body and the mind. We are simply open, open to the all-possible, open to the unknown. We can never go to it, because there is no one to go and nowhere to go. We can never take it, we can only be taken by it. So we must allow it.

We are accustomed to using the mind to understand, so we must go until the end of the mind, until it comes to the point of being completely exhausted. In other words, the mind must know its limits. This brings an absolutely relaxed state. The mind functions in space and time, but what we are profoundly is out of time. So time, the mind, can never understand what is beyond time. When the mind is exhausted, we are at the threshold of our real being. This threshold is a global feeling, free from any conceptualization. What is important is that when we say, "I have understood," we *feel* how the understanding has acted on us. Intellectual understanding dissolves in silence, and this silence is our real being. We may have a clear geometrical understanding in our mind, but this understanding is still objective; the geometrical understanding must completely dissolve in being understanding, which is a global feeling. It is really this global feeling that is meant when we speak of being the understanding.

Have you anything to say about it?

You said that when the mind sees its limits, it stops trying to grasp what it now knows is beyond it, and the energy is no longer outwardly directed. What then happens to this energy? Where does it go? How does its new deployment affect the physical body? In other words, where precisely is the energy in the state of waiting without waiting?

When there is no thinking, the energy is not directed and it returns to its globality. The physical body is relaxed, and in this relaxation there is no more hold for old patterns.

When we are taken by what we are, what role does the energy play?

Energy follows the thinking mind. It is the mind which directs energy. When the mind does not function and the body is relaxed, the energy is not wasted. It is contained and at one's disposal.

What do you mean exactly by geometrical understanding?

It is the clarity of the mind concerning truth. It is the clear perspective that truth is not objectifiable.

Do you mean, by geometrical understanding, that we see the "facts of reality," namely, that truth cannot be objectified, that it is beyond the mind, that an object only exists in consciousness, that truth can only be known by truth, and knowing these facts brings us to a kind of humility, openness, a forefeeling of truth itself?

Yes, all that we can call *smrti* belongs to a clear representation. The openness which comes with a clear understanding is like opening a curtain, and at a certain point there's the insight, the glimpse, which is the being understanding. Geometrical understanding is a higher reasoning, a reasoning which does not refer to objects but to the ultimate subject.

You have said that it is very rare for a mind to come to this geometrical clarity. Is this because only a few minds have the capacity for it? What are the abilities necessary for this clarity?

Geometrical clarity comes when there is a glimpse of truth. Potentially, everyone can have this glimpse. A clear mind is all that is required. By a clear mind I mean a mind that is completely free from expectation and anticipation. The mind must be open.

So one must live the truth in order to have a clear mind?

Yes. The glimpse must be there, the glimpse that the truth is not an object perceived.

When one has a clear perspective of truth, what is the next move, so that it dissolves into permanently being the understanding?

You must follow the understanding and live with it. Then you will see that every object is related to truth, has its potentiality in the truth, in consciousness. Remember what were the circumstances that brought the insight to you. It could be the sayings of the teacher, but it could also be some event in nature, as with Chuang Tzu or the Buddha, for example. So don't try to remember or regain the insight itself, but see again the circumstances leading to it and again feel how it acted in you, what physical effect it had on you, and live with this impact.

Is a clear geometrical understanding necessary for the insight?

In rare cases, it is not necessary, but it is important because it lends security to the insight. Insight based on feeling is shaky. It risks going into confusion. Experience and reasoning should be concomitant.

What brings the mind to clarity, the ability to have a clear relation to truth?

What is first, the driving power or discrimination? It is the driving power which brings the mind to discriminate. In other words, the felt is before the reasoning.

And what is felt? What is the driving power?

The global feeling, the feeling of beingness, of expansion, of being free from objects, from boundaries, a feeling of autonomy.

And how does the driving power cause the mind to be discriminating?

Because, as we said, the global feeling is the forefeeling of truth, and this foretaste inspires the mind to function on a higher level. It brings the mind to free itself from identifying truth with objects. Then the mind can go to the end. The mind is a car, and the petrol is the feeling, the driving force.

What kind of feeling is global feeling?

It is a feeling without a feeler. It is not in subject-object relationship. Do you see what I mean?

How can I come to this global feeling?

First, you may feel as if there is a lack in you. Perceive this feeling of living as fraction, accept it, let it be completely feeling. In accepting it you are completely open to it, without escaping and without directing it. This accepting and consequent openness is a glimpse of global feeling. It is a forefeeling of what you are fundamentally. Give yourself completely to this forefeeling. By this I mean, follow it to its source as a shadow brings you to its tree. In the same way, when the admirer gives himself completely to the admired, there is a moment when he feels himself lost in the admired, where there is no longer an admirer and something admired, there is only being. But this feeling must be paralleled by the mind. By this I mean that the mind must be aware of the perspective, the perspective which goes beyond the mind. The mind must know what it is not, what we are not: body, senses and mind. Only when the mind is thus informed can we speak of a really integrated understanding.

If I understand you correctly, at least intellectually I can understand that we are this consciousness, we are awareness. But this presupposes something which we understand as life, to be aware. I would like to know if reality exists without life. If I could hypothesize a world without life, without humanity, would there be reality?

You are the timeless when you really understand what is time. The thinking mind is time. All that is in succession creates time. This succession, time, is in the timeless. It is because you are in the timeless that you can conceive time. You can never perceive the timeless because it is not an object. You can only be it. It is your globality. It can never be known, because there is no longer a knower. If it could be objectified, it would not be globality. My answer comes a little from the back door.

Excuse me for insisting, but I am trying to understand whether or not there can be reality without life, without someone to be aware of it.

You are using the words "reality," "life," "aware," very loosely. Be clear about what is life, what is consciousness and what is an expression of consciousness. The expressions of consciousness exist, are perceived in consciousness, but consciousness is not in its perceiving. Life, consciousness, reality, is autonomous. This means it does not need a knower to be known. It is its own knowing. There are not two, there is only one. There is not a perceiver and something perceived. There is not a doer and something done. You are nowhere. You are nothing. The mind is simply a vehicle which appears in consciousness.

You know moments in daily life when you are completely absent as somebody. You can never think the absence, you just are absent. When you take yourself for somebody, you make yourself an object, and in daily life you are related from object to object. Then you occupy a fraction of yourself, and a fraction can only see a fraction.

7

Seeing a fraction can only bring reaction, and reaction can only create conflict. But when you are free from yourself, free from the idea of being somebody, in this absence of yourself, you are really presence, global presence. Then you see the surroundings, without reference, from your totality, from your globality, and there is no more reaction, there is only action. There is no entity in the cosmos. There is only functioning. There is not a functioner.

Are there levels of globality?

There are no levels in consciousness.

You said that there is no doer. What is it that makes us think we are doing?

We create the thinker. We project it. We are the creator, and we project the world at every moment. We create the world the moment we think of it. The world was never created. We create the world from moment to moment.

You say we are not the doer, but we are the creator. What's the difference?

The doer as authorship is only a fiction in the mind. There is no doer, there is nothing done, there is only doing. In the absence of an "I-concept" there is only spontaneous creation. It is only in the absence of yourself that there can be spontaneity and creativity. When you are free from intention, free from anticipation, free from attaining, free from the "I-image," when you are free from the becoming process, free from psychological memory, then you are really in the present; all doing comes out of the present and is related to this presence. Otherwise, you never live in the present, but go from past to future, from future to past.

In what way does it help to be free from the past when it remains only an observation?

See how the right observation changes the patterns in your body-mind. See the effect it has on you to *be* the observation.

When you think of the past, it is the present, a present thought. So in reality there is no psychological past. There is a chronological past, but this is a very small percentage of what we call "the past." Ninety percent of the so-called past is psychological and therefore fictitious. The psychological past is only for maintaining the "I-concept," and the "I-concept" is created entirely from memory. Most of our so-called memory is psychological. It maintains the security, the survival of the "me," of the "I." When you see, really, that the "I," the "me," has no existence in itself, that it is a thought, then psychological memory is given up. Enormous energy and tension are employed in thinking about, and maintaining, a psychological past. When we see that this is only day-dreaming, we give it up and there is a sudden, profound letting go, a deep relaxation, which brings us to a state of openness. Free from the "I-image" and psychological memory, we are open to intelligence, to a purely functional memory, a cosmic memory, a universal memory.

We can only know what we are not, we can never know

what we are, because we are the knowing. See, in the moment itself, how this understanding acts on you: that you can never know it, can never represent it; that you can only be it. Then there is a natural, an inevitable giving up. It is a transformation of energy. Something happens in your body, in your brain cells, and a moment comes when you feel that you are nothing, and you feel yourself in this nothingness. In this nothingness there is fullness.

You have said that the moment of waking up in the morning is very important. Can you say why?

Take note that the waking up belongs only to the body. First the body wakes up, and then the world, because the world only consists of sense perceptions and conceptions. So before the world wakes up, the body must be there. But before the body wakes up, you are. You are presence. The waking up of the body and the waking up of the world, the creation of the world, take place in you, in your presence.

In deep sleep there is not a knower. It is a state without a knower. In this way it is nearer to our real nature, the non-state, than the waking state and dreaming state, which suppose a knower. All three states are superimposed on reality, on consciousness. Before you go to sleep in the evening, give up all your qualifications, let dissolve all that is psychological, all residues of thought, ideas, problems, tensions and so on, so that there remains only one quality, the being without any quality. In other words, come to know what is impermanent in you, and what is permanent shines. The letting go of all that is impermanent, all that you are not, is the same giving up as in the moment when you pass away. When you die, you must, in any case, give up all your qualifications. And when you die you must give them up knowingly. Why wait till then? Why not die every evening so that you see that there is no death. When you have completely died in the evening, you will find yourself already present in the morning *before* the body wakes up. This is a very important moment. For then you will be convinced that the background of consciousness is never affected by the appearing of the three states.

Sometimes in the morning when I am not completely awake in the everyday mind, many creative ideas come to me. Is this the same state as you are talking about?

There is a transitional state where the subject-object relationship appears but is not fixed. It is a very creative state, the most creative for the artist, because the mind is free from habitual patterns of behavior.

I would like you to say something more about the giving up of all our qualifications. It sounds easy, but in practice it is not.

Giving up is not a volitional act. In volition there is still somebody who gives up. To give up is intentional, but when there is deep understanding, there is spontaneous giving up. When I discover that the key is not in my pocket, I automatically give up looking for the key in my pocket. It is just a fact which I accept that the key is not in my pocket.

What then is the use of the body?

The body, like your intelligence, is a vehicle, and it is as ridiculous to identify yourself with this vehicle as it is to identify yourself with your car or your house. But find out what it really means to say, "What is the use of my body?" or, "I am not the body." Before you can say, "I am not the body," you must first ask, "What is the body?" Otherwise, "I am not the body" remains an abstraction. Practically speaking, become aware of what your body is, how it presents itself to you. You are the knower of the body, so become aware of all the fear, anxiety, tension, reaction, aggression and so on in the body. How do fear, desire, all kinds of tension manifest themselves in my body? Get acquainted with all the reactions and compulsions in your daily life. It is vitally important to know your mechanism, not only as concept, but in the sensations of daily life, in everyday situations with your wife, your children, or your neighbor. It is very important.

Is it true that through being conscious of the body I am helped to become conscious that I am not the body?

It is the only way. Be aware of the way you function. Be aware how the moment you feel fear or anxiety and before you think, "I am afraid or anxious," there is the sensation of it on the level of the body. When you think, "I am afraid," you are no longer in the fear because you have conceptualized the perception. The moment the perception is conceptualized it is already memory, and when you live in the memory you can do nothing about the fear. So face it in its actuality. Become aware of where it is localized in your body, in your stomach or chest or neck or jaw; then you are in the present. In other words, let go of the concept "fear," because it belongs to the past, and face the actual fear before you name it. It is a very high art, to face a sensation without controlling it, escaping from it, analyzing or judging it, but simply listening to it. It is in this listening that you come to the understanding that you are not the body.

That last sentence struck me. Could you say more about it? Is it, as you say, in the listening that we come to know we are not the body, or is it through the listening?

It appears in listening. In listening there is no listener. It is not a function. Listening is awareness where no one is aware. The listening we are speaking about is unconditioned listening.

Did I understand you to say that during the course of the day there are moments of absence, only they are perceived after the fact?

There are moments in daily life where there is an absence of all activity. But we generally interpret this absence of activity to be just that—an absence of activities. We do not know it for what it is, presence or reality. This is because we identify awareness with objects and do not know objectless consciousness. It is like a white sheet of paper on which you write. When you fix your eyes only on the writing, you lose the white sheet. But the white sheet is there before the writing. The mind knows nothing about this absence of absence, because it functions habitually in subject-object relationship. But it is enough that the mind is informed that there is something beyond it. You know yourself only from below, above, left, right, in front and behind, in six directions. Then somebody says to you, "There is a seventh direction." The mind does not know what this is but, once informed of its existence, is open to it. In fact, the seventh direction is the heart, from whence all the directions start. It is enough to be open to it.

In connection with this—being open without knowing what we are open to—would you say something about what you call waiting without waiting?

You know yourself only in knowing. When you occasionally feel yourself in not-knowing, in this moment there is still in you an urge to eventually know. In the waiting of which we are speaking there is nothing to wait for, because there is no one to wait for it. So all the eccentric energy comes to a standstill, and you automatically come to a state of waiting without waiting for anything. Waiting for something belongs to the mind. But waiting free from waiting for anything does not belong to the mind. It belongs to our timelessness. And now I will tell you the most profound secret. In this waiting without waiting you will find that you are what you are waiting for. The waiting is itself the answer.

Has the subject-object relationship any use at all?

Subject-object relationships are on the level of the mind. The mind functions in subject-object relationship, but the mind is only a fraction of our functioning. It is one sense organ. When you perceive a flower, it is through the five senses. The mind has not yet come in. In the functioning of the five senses there is no subject or object. That comes later, when the perception gives way to conception and you say, "I see the flower," or "It is a rose," or "It has a lovely scent." Before those qualifications you and the flower are one in the act of pure perception. There is only seeing, there is only hearing when you hear a bird. Before you qualify the situation, there is not a hearer and nothing is heard, there is only hearing. When you afterwards think, "I hear the bird," or "I see the flower," you are no longer one with the seeing. You have conceptualized the act of seeing, and you no longer see the actual flower, but live in the concept, the name "flower." Sugar is not sweet. An apple is not the apple. Do you follow me? So, on the level of the mind there are subject-object relationships, but in your wholeness, your completeness, there is only seeing, asking, smelling, touching, hearing. Consciousness is one with its object.

What is love? What is the relation between love and being?

Love and being are not in relation. Relations exist only from object to object. We cannot say what love is in our relation with a flower, because love is not an object. You are love. And when you are really love, you can never not see love; everything is love. When you are love, you always see love. You may be far away from your lover and visualize him, his intelligence, beautiful eyes, sensitivity and so on, but there comes a moment, after you have gone through all his qualifications, when all that is left is a feeling of love. There is no more representation. But when you say, "I love him," you have again objectified the love.

When there is real understanding, it is not only on the level of the mind. There must be understanding in the psychosomatic body, too. This means the understanding must have time to abide and integrate in the body. And, as there is a biological memory, a body memory, of what the body is fundamentally, we should constantly be in a relaxed state, in a state receptive to the original body.

It is normal that the little child appropriate the world to itself. The child in the womb of the mother becomes aware of its immediate surroundings, temperature, heartbeat, fluid, etc. Once it leaves the mother's body, the child eagerly appropriates the outer environment in a kind of biological grasping, taking. It is a natural stage in the life of a human being. But there comes a transition where there is nothing more to take. There comes the deep understanding that there is nothing to take. However, our sense perceptions, eyes, ears and so on generally remain in an infantile state of grasping, taking, appropriating. So when we speak of the body being in the perceiving, the receiving state, we mean to knowingly give up all tension in the eyes and ears and all the sense organs, particularly the brain. The brain is also a sense organ which we can feel and relax. It is important to come to the relaxed state of the brain. Then when we have something to think, we think, and when there is no need to think, we don't think.

Would you talk a little bit about the relationship between a mother and her child?

16

To live in the idea of being a mother is fractional living. Someone who takes herself for a mother will take her child for a child, and this relation is fractional. Because the idea of being the mother hinders the absolute non-relationship.

When you are free from the concept "mother," you are really a mother. Then when circumstances call on you to be a mother, when the child asks for a mother, you are a mother. But don't live in mothering. You are nothing, and in this nothingness the mother comes and goes. Then there is a current of love.

This is another example of biological behavior being at odds with realized behavior, because to be a mother is often a biological act, as it is to be a father. Another biological behavior is to quickly complete an object with memory, a table, a tree or a lion. In the world of survival, such quick completion is essential. What can you say about this fact, that we must transcend our biology to come to our freedom?

The problem is not biology but psychology. To take yourself as a father, mother, lawyer or businessman is fractional living. Then you act according to certain patterns. When you are established in your wholeness, the father or mother appears in this wholeness. Similarly, conception, memory, is an essential tool of our brain, but to live in memory is the problem.

In India there is the tradition that a person should, ideally, go through the four stages of existence: brahmacharya (student), garhasthya (householder), vanaprastha (forest-dweller) and sannyasa (renunciant). What do you think of this tradition?

These stages belong to the progressive way and have nothing to do with the direct approach. Thinking like this hinders you from looking for what you really seek: to be free from all states and stages.

Could you talk to us about faith?

When you are really still—still means in not-knowing anything—that is really a blessed state.

How can I, right now, come to this blessed not-knowing state?

You can never come to it. In trying to come to it, you go away from it. This understanding is all you need to come to not-knowing. Live in this not-knowing.

When you live in understanding, what is your motive for doing?

When the doing is no longer done from the doer point of view, then there is only doing, spontaneous doing. But before we come to this spontaneous doing, we must be free from the doer. Otherwise, there is only reacting. So we must come to looking without naming, without interpretation, simply looking, hearing, smelling, touching, tasting. It is the situation which acts in us; action occurs according to the facts of the situation, which we can only see when there is no interference of an "I-concept," a "me." In this looking we are free from all luggage. It is very comfortable!

There is a problem that springs directly from having to trans-

late, namely, that in the modern Greek language there is no equivalent for saying "seeing, hearing, smelling."

How do you name the functioning of the senses?

In a multiple way, not with one word. But I think the meaning has been conveyed, because we've used words from ancient Greek. The question I wanted to ask is whether language itself, as it appears from this concrete example, is a limiting factor?

In a certain way we are conditioned by language, that is clear; but when you are creative, you can find the equivalent. But we must become free from language. We must make a new language.

When you say, "There is no seer, there is no seen, there is only seeing," that is difficult to translate. There is no one word that is acceptable in modern Greek. It is translated in what some people say is not very acceptable modern Greek. But I think what is more interesting is to create a new language, as you said.

There is a seer, there is something seen. Something seen is a happening. What is the Greek word for happening? In happening there is not a happener, there is only happening. I am sure you will find it.

Where does thought come from?

When thinking starts from thought, it is a defense, it is aggression. But when a thought starts from silence, then I

19

would say it is offering. It is thanking. Thanking for being allowed to be.

November 3, 1990, Afternoon

Feel deeply in you when there is attention to something, and when there is objectless attention. Objectless attention is your original non-state. It is meditation without a meditator and without anything to meditate on. But don't make this objectless attention an object. Don't localize it in the body. Don't think about it. It is neither outside nor inside. It has no border, it has no center.

Objectless attention is undirected attention. This directionless attention is the natural state of the completely relaxed, quiet mind. In a certain way this directionless attention appears to come from behind you, in the small brain area, whereas directed attention comes from in front in the region of the forehead. But, ultimately, objectless attention has no localization. An apparent localization behind is a transitionary phase, an important pedagogical device, to take you away from the thought factory in the forehead.

When the mind is relaxed, objects appear and disappear, thoughts appear and disappear in this directionless attention. Awareness remains after the disappearance of the object and is there before it. The awareness then is not a state you go in and out of, but the non-state in which objects come and go. Awareness, objectless attention, conscious-

21

ness, is the only constant. It is the background behind every perception. It is the light which gives life to all objects.

So make it clear for yourself when attention is directed towards something and when that something disappears in undirected attention.

You may have some questions.

Then why don't we touch objectless attention all the time?

Because you go away from it. The mind thinks that when there is absolute, objectless stillness, it is only an absence, an absence of activity. Let me give you an analogy. You have been going into a room very often and you're accustomed to seeing a carpet. But one day the carpet is sent to the cleaner, and when you come into the room, what do you see? Do you see the floor? No, you see the absence of the carpet! So you must come to the absence of the absence. Do you follow?

Yes.

When this absence becomes an object and you are aware of it, where should attention go? Where should the emphasis be?

Be aware that you face an object, because the absence is also an object and is still perceptible by the mind. Real presence is when the absence, as an object, dissolves, and there is a true emptiness of all objects. This emptiness is fullness. But what happens when the teaching is progressive, when you follow a progressive path, is that you become locked in a subject-object relation, because you have spent a lot of time and energy in stilling the mind, purifying the body, attaining subtle states and so forth, and all this takes place with an observer, a doer, a witness. You have attempted to come to that which is timeless by working through time. As a result, you become so accustomed to being in the subject-object, observer-observed relationship, where there is always an end in view, a subtle object, that you cannot let go of the last object, the state of the absence of objects. And you are trapped in the emptiness of the state and do not know its fullness. From time to time one can use elements which belong to progressive teaching to purify the body-mind, but only with the deep conviction that what you are fundamentally can never be an object. Because the real teaching has nothing to do with the mind. It points directly to the ultimate. In this way one sees that there is nothing to teach. All that is teachable belongs to the mind.

What do you mean by "conviction"? How can I come to it?

Conviction comes when you inquire and suddenly see that all that you are looking for is an object. Then the striving energy returns to its homeground. In the state of conviction you see that there is nothing to attain. It is a state of openness where you live in not-knowing. Truth can never be objective.

I would like you to talk more about this. I have spent twenty years on a progressive, so-called spiritual path, and even before that I was conditioned to achieve and attain. Yet now you tell me I must "have the deep conviction" that what I am can never be an object. I believe you and love you and feel deep emotion when I hear your sayings, but how can I have the conviction that will break the bad habits of a lifetime?

Believe that you are the ultimate, the light which gives life to all objects. First believe what I tell you, then make it your own. You have the right to ask me how I came to be convinced and to follow my instructions. There must be listening. Conviction is a feeling, not a mental representation. Be open to the seventh direction.

Sri Atmananda Krishna Menon talked about consciousness and functional consciousness. What did he mean?

All is perceived by consciousness in consciousness. Consciousness is not affected by function. Functional consciousness is consciousness in relation with objects.

I would like to ask about meditation in relation to children. If a child meditates with a mantra, does it do any good, or is it bad for him?

It is not good or bad. But it is more appropriate for the child to know more about the vibrations and currents in his body. In discovering this he becomes attentive, and being attentive brings him, one day, to a feeling of distance from his object of observation. He comes to a space relation where he is no longer stuck, bound, to the object. And certainly he will, one day, feel himself in this objectless observation.

A mantra in itself has no meaning. Its value lies in the pronunciation, the vibration. Our body is built of vibration. Each organ in the body has its special sound. Medical science will, in future, certainly come to healing through sound. When there is right pronunciation of the mantra, our body is affected by this vibration, and we come to a very deep, relaxed state where there is no directed attention and therefore no longer an observer and something observed; there is only being.

But the right pronunciation of a mantra takes years, maybe a whole lifetime, and you can have the same results in a more direct way. The body has an organic memory of its natural, unconditioned state. Once you have experienced this relaxed, light body, it will solicit you often and remind you when it is not relaxed. Knowing that, you will soon be able to go immediately into this absolutely relaxed state. Of course, there is still an observer and an observed— the relaxed body. But there comes a moment when there is a convergence of observer and observed. Then there is oneness. That is the "I am." There is nothing wrong with a mantra, but there may be the danger that you become bound to the mantra. As the ultimate goal is to be free, free from everything, free from yourself, completely autonomous, bound to nothing, belonging to nothing, then why take a path which may well lead you to being bound to something? When you are bound to something, you are in duality.

The ultimate teaching is to make yourself free, free from yourself, free from what you are not. Free from the teacher, because in the end there is nothing to teach and, as there is nothing to teach, there cannot be a teacher. There is only a current of love—call it friendship, or anything you want. But there is no longer any object relationship.

I would like to know more about the organic memory you mentioned.

The body is built of energy. In observing the body, you will actually feel, have the sensation, of different levels of energy. It is a perception. It may appear solid, or fluid, or appear as air. It may appear as light. All these qualities are evoked, and finally you come to the feeling that your body is only light. The nature of the body is transparent. When you come to the purely transparent feeling of your body, that is the healing body.

Is the organic body the light body or the relaxed body?

The organic body is the light body. The simply relaxed body is a dead body, a passive body. The organic body is alert, sensitive, elastic, ready at any moment for right functioning. When the body is only relaxed, you are lost in the relaxation. This is a passive or lazy state. But the light body is in awareness. So be very aware of the relaxed body. When you are aware of it, you find yourself no longer in it. In this awareness there is a transference from the object, the body, to the subject, awareness. Then the body, freed from its objectivity, appears in awareness as light, pure energy.

You said that the relaxed body will solicit us and we will be able to go directly to the relaxed state, but that this state is still in subject-object relationship. Then you said that at some point there is a convergence of observer and observed. So the question is: how does a subject-object relationship dissolve into oneness? What is the condition for this convergence?

It is the subject which keeps the object alive. When the subject gives up its looking for a goal, then it disappears, and with it, the object.

If consciousness is one, why is there the play of the many?

It seems as though there are many when you identify with a fraction, when you take yourself for what you are not. But "why" questions never bring satisfaction. I would say, put aside the why.

What is the purpose of objects? What is lila?

An object only exists, is perceived, because there is perceiving. If one can talk of a mission for the object, it is only to reveal this perceiving. As we said, when the ego-subject lets go of all qualification, it disappears and the object, as object, disappears, revealing the ultimate subject, the perceiver. In reality this is the same as perceiving. An object is meaningful only when it points to its origin, the perceiving. Then it is sacred. Otherwise, it is profane.

Is lila this play of objects pointing to the subject, the sacred play, or is it the phenomenal world, the profane play?

Lila, the divine play, does not come from the object itself. It comes from silence. In other words, it is creative. Otherwise, when the object comes from another object, thought, it is repetition. Thought which springs from thought is not creative. Creative thought springs from silence, not-knowing. It is not conditioned. *Lila* does not refer to the phe-

27

nomenal world. It refers to the movement of beauty in Beauty.

If I am already fundamentally free, then why do I not feel as though I am free?

The only obstacle is your belief that you are an independent entity. That is the only obstacle. You are stuck in this belief. It belongs to a personality invented by society, education, experience, beliefs, second-hand information and all kinds of reading. You have identified yourself with this fictitious "I" and you live from this point of view. You look at and contact the surroundings from this viewpoint. Because the personality is an object like any other, you live in object-object relationship.

What happens when you become aware of it? The moment you become aware of it is the most important opportunity, an opportunity to see how this insight acts on you. Until now your brain has functioned in the pattern of taking yourself for someone, and when this pattern suddenly collapses there is a reorchestration of all your energy, a transformation of your being. The old reflex, which is so deep-rooted, may come up from time to time, but you are now aware of it. You ignore it and then forget it. Why put yourself in the cage of a fraction? You are the whole, the global.

Is this insight—that you have taken yourself for someone— enlightenment, or is it a forefeeling?

This insight frees the mind from wrong thinking. It comes

from your real nature. Often the mind appropriates the insight again, and it appears as a point, an experience in space and time. The insight itself is constant.

Is the insight that you are not the personality the ray of light in the dark room?

Yes, but you are still in the dark room, even though there is light in it. You must give yourself entirely to this light, and it will take you towards its source. Then there will be a sudden moment when you are no longer in the dark at all but are completely taken by the light. This was my experience.

The mind is identified with objects, but it governs. Is there something, other than simply being open, to help the mind let go of its hold?

The natural state is a non-state of not-knowing, non-concluding. When there is knowing, there is a state. But your real nature is not-knowing. It is a total absence of all that you think you are, which is all that you are not. In this total absence of what you are not, there is presence. But this presence is not yours. It is the presence of all living beings.

You must not try to be open. You are open. When you say, "I must be open," you create a state. When you say, "I am going to meditate," you make a state of it. You *are* meditation. When you go into the state of so-called meditation or openness, you are like a donkey in a stall.

What is intelligence?

Intelligence is spontaneous behavior. It is creativity. When you are free from the person, from the "I-concept," when you are free from psychological memory, then you are open to intelligence. This intelligence is in you, it is not outside.

Then is there no such thing as a person being more intelligent or less intelligent?

When you are intelligent, there is no quantity or quality to that intelligence. It is right acting. By right acting I mean letting the situation tell you what it needs, not your telling the situation what it needs. When you stay out of the picture and patiently wait for the facts to unfold, you will undoubtedly be surprised by what the situation tells you. Then you will act spontaneously without the premeditation that accompanies the ego. This spontaneity does not go through the discriminating mind. Nor can it be confused with impulsiveness, which only apparently does not go through the discriminating mind, but which is founded on old patterns of behavior, reactions. Spontaneous, intelligent acting occurs naturally the moment there is pure perception, perception without conceptualizing.

In many of the teachings of different traditions and philosophical systems, we are encouraged to live with a certain amount of measure in our lives. For example, nothing in excess, the Middle Way and so on. Or we are told to pursue a certain diet or way of life. What do you think about this?

On the physiological level, one could say you are what you absorb. As soon as you come more in contact with the workings and sensations of your body-mind, you will see how the things you absorb act on you. You will notice how what you take in, not only by the mouth but also through the skin, affects how you wake up in the morning, how the body feels to you in the morning. You will be interested in how the body appears to you before going to sleep at night, or after a nap in the afternoon. But all this calls for observation, not the concentration of a hunting dog, but a relaxed observation without any intention. Then, in this observation free from reaction, you will act intelligently. Where you feel a lack you will make an addition of certain elements, and where you feel a heaviness you will omit certain things, until you come to the organic body, where the expanded, light, energy body is freed. No system can bring you to know yourself in this way. Only reaction-free observation, seeing the facts as they are.

All this is on the level of observation. Simply observe in openness, and you will come to the right way.

What is the role of sex in life?

When you love someone and are, yourself, love, you will see in the other only love. And there may come a moment, which you cannot project, when you would like this oneness to be expressed also on the level of body feeling. It is a pure act of love. Making love must be understood in this way; otherwise, it is a deviation. But it is not necessary that true love come to a sex relation. The oneness can be expressed in a look, a touch, a scent.

By deviation do you mean it is an act of pleasure, a kind of escape, and not an expression of the joy of oneness?

When you look for pleasure, there is also pain.

What about making love to have children? Is that a deviation?

No, if it is to make the oneness concrete in a certain way. A child ideally is the result of oneness where there is no lover or beloved, only love.

If love, where there is no lover or beloved, is timeless, then from the ultimate, not social, point of view, can it not be a timeless moment of oneness even when there is no long-standing relationship?

I agree perfectly. But where there is intention, to have pleasure or to make a child, oneness is not expressed, because there is still a duality—someone wanting something. There is tension and anticipation. And it is interesting that often the child does not appear, because the love is hindered from full expression.

What do you think of religious traditions which say one must only make love to make children and not for any other reason?

There's not a "must." When there is a moment to show love, it is spontaneous behavior, and this spontaneous behavior is right behavior.

When is art true art? Is it when it doesn't have a purpose or a cause?

First, let us be clear about what art is. The producer of art is, I would say, in a thanking position. I say a thanking position because he thanks for being allowed to be. Being allowed to be in this joy, in this equanimity, brings him to produce art and to share this joy with others. So art, in a certain way, points directly to our real nature.

The science of creating art is to free our expression from the material part. By this I mean that the creation should take us beyond the five senses. It must free us from matter and also from ideas. Art must be conceived in such a way that it meets the observer. To do this, to come to this meeting with others, there must be room for the observer to participate. This means one must know exactly where to stop. When you know really where to stop, what not to put, there is a coming together of the artist and the person who looks at it, because the observer is invited to participate, to complete the work. This is true of painting, music, architecture, poetry, dance. This coming together is the goal, if we can speak of a goal, of the work of art.

So when there are too many words or images, when the work is too busy, the observer has no room left to be creative?

Exactly. There must be space in the work, and this space can only appear when the artist as "an artist" is absent. When the artist puts himself into the work, it ceases to be art and becomes a piece of self-expression, often suitable only for discussion on the analyst's couch. When there is no one writing or painting, there will automatically be an economy of expression. Look how a couple of images in a few lines of haiku poetry can evoke a whole realm of emotion in the reader. That is an example of what I mean.

If we can give an example from the theatre, at what point should the actor stop, to have this coming together with the spectator?

It depends what kind of play you present. But, in any case, the actor must take the audience with him. He must not dominate them with his personality or his technique. It belongs to the high art of the actor to give the right amount of stimulation. If he gives too little, his role is bland like a tasteless dish. If he gives too much, the audience is nauseated. The actor gives the audience the opportunity to be creative and to complete it. In completing it there is the joy of creating together. So the member of the audience finds himself in a passive-active state. He listens and at the same time he completes what has knowingly not been revealed. Art is to express the inexpressible.

By not expressing it....?

Yes. When there is no interference from the "I," there is economy of expression. But too much economy of expression is also interference, because there's too much volition in it. Not interfering is interfering.

What is happiness?

When you say, "I am happy," you are not happy, because in this moment you have created a state of happiness. When you are actually happy, you don't think of saying, "I am happy," because in that moment of happiness there is not a knower of the happiness, and you are in your glory, your wholeness, your globality. Happiness is causeless. You think that it has a cause—a lovely car, a beautiful woman, a lot of money, a nice house, a prestigious job. But when you look deeply, you will find that when you are actually in happiness, there is just happiness with nobody who is happy and no cause of the happiness. This is your real nature. What hinders you to live your real nature, happiness, is that, knowingly or unknowingly, you project a cause.

Many desires come up in daily life and bring me continual agitation. How should I deal with these desires?

When you look really deeply into the motive for your actions in daily life, you will see that they are generally for the survival of the "I-concept," the person. It is important to be aware of this. When you really feel in you the desire to be happy, totally follow this desire. Fundamentally, all desire leads to the one source of desire, the desire to be desireless, to be free from desire. But we must follow desire like we follow the shadow projected by a tree. It leads to the tree.

Can we distinguish types of desire, or is desire one?

The desire comes from what you most desire. To be the self comes from the self. When you follow the desire, there comes a kind of reorchestration of the energy where all dispersed energy becomes centered. So it is useless to say,

"You must be like this, you must be like that." This or that are the result of experience, deeper experience.

It is a fact that we are identified with what we call the gross body, because if a person dear to us dies, we often cannot overcome the grief, the loss. What can you say about this?

The person, before dying, must become free from the body-mind. If the person is not, in daily life, really free from the body-mind, it is very difficult to be free when the ultimate moment comes to pass away. The people around the person who is dying can be an obstacle, because family and friends retain a hold on the personality and won't let the dying one go. This applies not only to those present, but to those absent. Very often, the family is an obstacle.

Sometimes, in meetings like this, questions come up in me which remain incomplete and cannot be expressed. Could you say something about this?

When your question does not come to formulation, just be still. It is only in your stillness that the question can become clear.

Is it important, then, that the question become clearly formulated?

Yes. But do not anticipate an answer. Keep to the question, then you will be open to the answer. The verbal answer can only be a suggestion. The formulated answer is never a total answer. The answer as we understand it on the intellectual level must abide in silence. It must abide in awareness. Then it is completely understood. What appears is the question, but what does not appear will be the answer. Live completely this absence of formulation. On the level of the mind we use symbols, but we must come to what the symbols symbolize. When we have a question, we must live in the questioning feeling and not force it to a conclusion. If we try to understand it through memory, the past, it will never give us the total answer. When you live with the question in lovingness, not touching it, not forcing it, it is like a child, who one day maybe will tell you its secret.

What is it that can help us to discern between the answer at the level of the mind and the answer that comes from silence?

The understanding that comes from the mind is still in conflict. Understanding that comes from silence returns to knowing yourself in silence.

There must not be any wishful thinking in your listening. You must accept the facts. The solution is in the facts, and the answer is also in the facts. Accepting facts means seeing things as they are. In this unqualified acceptance of the facts, the truth unfolds. It unfolds in your accepting, which is a global feeling. The mind can only be clear when it is grounded in your wholeness, your globality. Otherwise, the mind functions in fractions. You can only really know the facts from your totality, where there is not a knower, not a fraction, there is only knowing. Sometimes the ego comes up and questions the wholeness and throws you again into doubt. You should not fall into the trap.

Would you not say that doubt, a certain skepticism, is a very important tool which prevents one from falling into beliefs?

No. Skepticism is anticipation. How can you come to understanding by projecting a result? In doubt you can never become happy. Falling for one belief system after another comes from a lazy mind that is looking for a quick solution. An inquiring, not a skeptical, mind is the only tool necessary.

In many schools or teachings it is said that we must help our fellow humans. Often this "must" doesn't come automatically to the person. What is your opinion?

The "must" is never spontaneous. When life asks for help, help. But don't become a "must helper," a professional helper.

The ideal is to help spontaneously. But until we reach that point, isn't the "must" a useful way to it?

The "must" makes you a dull and stupid person. Free yourself from the "must." When a child falls down, you don't think, "Shall I pick her up?" You just do it. When you are thirsty, you just get a drink of water. Don't make a problem in life where there is no problem.

Sometimes help entails a psychological cost.

Who suffers?

The one who tries to help.

But who suffers? Find out who. Who is this me? Only an object can suffer, but you are not an object. You know the suffering, you are the knowing of the suffering.

But I have not reached that point where I am the knower of the suffering.

You haven't understood. Perhaps tomorrow morning you will understand.

Please talk to us about what is called satsang.

First tell me what you understand by *satsang*.

The usual meaning of the word is that you are in good company, near someone who is blessed.

But it depends completely on the stand which you take. From the level of the mind, the level of the "me," you are never in good company. You are constantly in "I want, I need, I must." From here you can never be, or have, good company, because good company starts with yourself. A teacher doesn't take himself for a teacher. He or she gives without asking for anything. He takes himself for nothing, and in this way he awakes nothingness in you when he says, "You are nothingness." That is real togetherness. That is perfect company.

You said the teacher asks for nothing. Has the teacher then no hope or expectation of the disciple?

For the teacher all is possible. He teaches what life asks for in the moment itself. He does not anticipate any result. He is completely in the present.

What is it that a teacher most wants in his disciple?

That he is free from himself. Then there is togetherness in love.

And what are the qualities of a good disciple?

Eagerness. The profound desire to be free from himself, the personality, all that he or she is not. One must be ripe to look for freedom. See how much energy you spend in making money or in pleasing your lover or in showing off your personality. Look how much energy you spend in order to be admired. Begin by giving a fraction of this eagerness to self-inquiry, and you will see what a beautiful taste it has. This beauty will solicit you and take you beyond all expectations.

Is the person wrong who wants to do many things in life?

What is the goal in doing many things? What is the motive to do many things? Don't you see in the moment itself what nonsense it is? *Alors. . . .*

You may want to do many things because you like to do many things. It is not necessarily an illness.

It is merely an escape, because you have not become profoundly oriented and so you feel bored.

What is spiritual greed? The need to learn more and more?

Will you make the point here that certain things are not spiritual? All things are spiritual, and all things are beauty.

If what man is looking for is in him, why has he forgotten about it? Why is it not realized every day?

Again the why! There is nothing spiritual or not spiritual. All is spiritual. Everything becomes spiritual the moment it refers to its background, to silence. It is silence which makes an object sacred. It is sacred when it refers to ultimate awareness. Then it ceases to be an object, because it is an expression of consciousness, an extension of consciousness. Don't forget it; there are not two, there is only one.

November 4, 1990, Morning

When we are free from thinking, as happens often in daily life, there is no time. Time is the mind, but our real nature is beyond the mind. It is in the timeless that time appears; otherwise, how could we speak of time? We are the timeless; we live the timeless in the now. In other words, we are presence in the present. We can never think of the present, because we are the present. When we think of the present, it is already the past. So we can only think of the past. Time is created by the succession of thoughts, but when we live in the now we are constantly one with the object. In the now, we live our verticality; otherwise, we live on the horizontal plane, which is psychological time.

What about chronological time: Monday, Tuesday, Wednesday, the change of the seasons and the becoming old of the body? This is also on the horizontal plane.

Chronological time is always in the now. By this I mean that chronological time only has reality when it meets the vertical. Functional time, succession and creation, only exist by and through the vertical.

What hinders us from living the now?

We can only live the now when we are free from being identified with the person. When we live in the personality, we live in psychological survival because the personality needs situations, needs time, to exist.

Even when one lives in the present, the body gets old and there is death to face.

When you live in the now, there's the conviction that there's no death because in the now there is only life. So before you speak of death, first ask yourself the question, "What is life?" Begin with life. When there is real understanding, the being understanding of life, the problem of death doesn't come into the picture. The machine, the tool, our body, becomes used, but life was never born so can never die.

But on the level of the body and the mind we are born and die.

When you say, "I am born," do you know really what you are saying? Have you experienced that you are born? Your mother said that you were born at half past three on Wednesday. It is recorded in the town hall, but all that is second-hand information from your mother. I am sure that when you inquire really deeply, you will never discover your birth, because fundamentally you are life, you are consciousness, consciousness behind all objects, consciousness behind all situations. When you were two, five, seventeen, twenty-four, at every moment it was and is the same consciousness.

When I was two, or five, or ten, this consciousness existed. Did it exist before?

Absolutely! Before you were born. What is the meaning, really, to be born?

It means I have the experience of the world.

You never asked to be born. You will not ask to die, or to have an illness. It is a happening to you. You cannot make the choice whether to die or not. You are not free at all. You cannot choose your illness. All this happens. The only real freedom you have is to be your timeless self, so the only reason for your existence is to find this out. But you cannot find what you are, because you are it. The eye cannot see its seeing. So you can only inquire into what you are not. Real birth is not the birth which is the result of two people; real birth is when you come to know what you are, when you wake up in yourself. Otherwise, you remain an accident until the end of your life.

If we have no choice, does this mean that all events in our lives are predestined, whether or not we inquire into our real nature?

All is already on the film. What is not on the film is your being aware of it. You are the light which gives life to the film. When you ask, "Is all on the film?" you ask it from the point of view of time, and you put yourself in the film. But when I say, "All is on the film," I speak from the timeless, the light which gives life to the film.

Where does the question "Who am I?" spring from?

From the "I am" itself.

If life and death do not depend on us, why is it important, as we said yesterday, to be aware at the moment of death?

If there is a goal in this phenomenal life, it is to find out who we are. To be free means to be free from one's self, from what one is not. There comes a moment, in any case, when we must be free from what we are not. In the last breath before passing away, we may see in the moment itself what we really are not, and then live really what we are. So in a certain way one must prepare oneself for dying. But there is no need to wait till the last breath, because we die at every moment between inhalation-exhalation, exhalation-inhalation, thinking-free from thinking, free from thinking-thinking. At every moment our phenomenal existence dies in consciousness, in stillness. And we die every evening before going to sleep.

Is there any freedom of the will, even with regard to understanding who we are?

You are only free when you understand what you are; then you are free from what you are not. Otherwise, you are bound to what you are not, and your life becomes a problem. You can only know what you are not. What you are, you can never know, because there is not a knower of it. It is your globality, your totality.

Do we have a choice to understand what we are not, or is that also predetermined?

What you profoundly are is not on the film, so when you are free from the film you will be ultimately free. Otherwise, you remain bound to the film. So what is important is to know how to live with, how to deal with, the film. Knowing how to look at it is the highest art. Before you say, "I am not this or that," you must explore what it is that you are not. In this exploration, you feel already free from what you explore. You have a foretaste, a glimpse of freedom. All so-called freedom in our society really refers to this freedom.

I want to ask my question another way. Some years ago there was a crisis in my life which brought with it an insight, a forefeeling of my real being. For some time I lived in this forefeeling, but then the old patterns came back, and although my life is completely changed, I still do not live in my wholeness. Was the insight wasted on me? Have I lost a golden opportunity forever?

When there is an insight and you live this insight even for a moment, a timeless moment, it is not an ordinary event in your life. It brings already a change in your surroundings and activities. You see things from a new point of view which is not really a point but your globality. You must give all your love to it. That means that you must live in it, but not by trying to remember it. Rather, if the old patterns seem to come back, then reconstruct, visualize, the situation prior to the insight and not the insight itself. You will see that in this moment you were completely free from the person. Don't forget that this was not an experience like any other, because it was in the absence of the experiencer that the impact was so powerful. Every moment is a golden opportunity.

I understood you to say that it is important to be aware at the moment of death. What happens to those of us who die without this awareness?

In our ordinary language, one would say it was a waste of time being born, because you didn't use the opportunity to know yourself; you missed it. But enjoy yourself!

Doesn't the complete absence of freedom of the will cause a problem with regard to what happens after death, or even before death?

To be born as a human being and not a snake is already something tremendous. The galaxy, the moon, the sun, stones, animals, vegetables, all the universe has helped us to be what we are, just as we have helped them to be what they are. So, in a certain way, we should express our deep thanks to them for helping us to be a human being. But all this is more or less on the biological level. To be born human is to have an opportunity to know ourselves. I will keep my answer open and not go to the end of your question. You should go to the end.

Who is it, exactly, who observes? Who knows? What is observation?

There is not an observer, not a controller. There is only observing. On the level of the divided mind, there is an observer and something observed, but in the act of observation there is only observing

What happens after death?

If I spoke to you about what happens after death, there would be some speculation in it, but speaking from experience, I can affirm that death cannot touch what you are profoundly. You are not born and cannot die. When you realize your real nature, the question of death no longer concerns you.

I am sorry to keep coming back to the same point, but there is something I want to clarify. You said that we must have awareness at the moment of death. Otherwise, we waste the opportunity. . . .

To be born, yes.

Suppose we miss the opportunity. Are we born again as an animal or a snake?

As long as you take yourself for a personal entity, there is karma. But with regard to what we ultimately are, karma has no place. So don't think of karma, don't think of what does not ultimately concern you. You are the Self, that is all that is important to you. Direct your attention only to what you are. And you cannot deny that when you say, "I am," there is the strongest feeling. It gives you immediately a feeling of being free from all that you are not. Eventually the symbol "I am" will go away, and there will remain only the essence. All talk of after-death is speculation. In any case you will not miss the hierarchies of the angels!

Inside me there is no conflict, but outside there is. What can be done?

Is there really an outside and an inside? What you call inside is as much a perception as what you perceive on the so-called outside. What is the difference between the tension you are aware of in your body and the yellow flower? All is outside except you, who are the seer. That is a pedagogical way of talking, for in reality there is no outside nor inside. I don't think there is any problem in what you call the outside. It is in *how* you look at it. Try to change your way of looking at it. Be aware of the mechanism, of how you function.

You put life into categories and see your surroundings in patterns. It is only the "I," the "me," which creates categories for its own security, for survival. So change your way of looking at things. Begin at the earliest possible moment. When you go back to your room, try to look at it like a child who is seeing, for the first time, the stars in the sky. Look at your table, your chair, your bed, your bookshelves, how they are placed in the space of your room. You may decide to change the position of your bed. But only this new, creative way of looking where there is no selection can bring you to change the position of your bed. When you do not see things globally, but with your head, you objectify them; you see them isolated, and this gives rise to insecurity. The thinking process is a defense against this insecurity. It is from this region, your forehead, that the publication of objects starts. Try once to look at your room, your surroundings, from behind you. Don't now ask me how to do it, but try to understand what I mean by looking at things from behind. You will immediately see that you feel your globality, and in this globality one object is in relation to another object, and there can be no conflict.

What does "God" mean?

It is a concept. Free yourself from the concept. Be what you are fundamentally. There you will find the answer: God is when you are not. It is only in your absence of being somebody that you come to feel what It is, what He is.

It was said yesterday that the thought that springs from silence is thanks for being allowed to be. My question is, when we say, "for being allowed to be," is that a way of speaking, or how can we understand it?

It is thanking that you are happiness.

Is the happiness always present, and sometimes we are aware of it and sometimes not?

It is the background and the support of all appearings. It is ours. Be only aware that you go away from it.

Does that mean that we are identified with this happiness and then it already becomes the past?

When you are in the state or, more precisely, the non-state of happiness, you don't know that you are happy, because there is not a knower in happiness. You simply are happiness, and there is not an agent there to know it. The Self, happiness, knows itself by itself.

Your happiness is not dreaming. Whatever is not happiness is dreaming.

We said before that it is a waste of energy to look for ourselves. Do we then just turn towards ourselves?

To look for something is to project energy, eccentric energy. It is so interesting to see that eighty percent of your activity in daily life is spent in projecting tremendous energy for the survival and changing of what you are not. When you see to what lengths you have gone to preserve what you are not, you will smile.

So we do nothing?

Don't think about doing or not doing. When you see it clearly, that makes you straight.

Straight?

The energy is no longer dispersed, it is contained, and you feel yourself in your verticality, the correct inner position.

November 4, 1990, Afternoon

Silence, the stillness of which we are speaking, does not belong to the mind. The mind is a functional tool which works in discontinuity. So from time to time the mind can be still, but the nature of the mind is function. Conscious- ness, silence, stillness, is a continuum. This continuum is not affected by the functional mind.

There are moments in life when there is no anticipation or thinking about the past, when we spontaneously live in silence. But because we only know ourselves in activity and are not informed otherwise, we take the silent moment for an absence, an absence of activity. Then, because we do not know the silence behind activity, when we follow the inner need to be still or to meditate, we get stuck on the level of the mind as we try not to think, try to empty the mind of objects in an effort to create silence. But this absence of activity is also an object. Many books have been written about stilling the mind, stilling thoughts, but all this is effort, a waste of energy. A disciplined mind can never be a free mind.

When we are invited to meditate, we can go into medi- tation as we go into a laboratory, on the condition that we already know that the meditator is the stuff of the mind, a mind which is looking for an experience of God, or beauty, or silence. In the realization that the mind can never reach what is beyond it, the meditator has no more role to play, and there is no object of meditation. When this is profoundly understood, there is a spontaneous giving up of the reflex to try to experience what is beyond experience, and one is in meditation, continual meditation. Understanding is the only way to reach beyond the mind.

In meditation without a meditator there is no introversion or extroversion. There is a popular image in India of a monkey covering its eyes, nostrils and ears in an attempt to meditate, and there is another monkey laughing at him. The organs—seeing, hearing, tasting, smelling, touching— go on functioning until the end of our life, but this has nothing to do with meditation. In meditation the eyes are open, but there is nothing seen; there is what could be called a sense of visibility. There is hearing, but there is nothing heard; there is audibility, and so on. In other words, there is seeing and hearing, without a specific object seen or heard. But the background, silence, continues.

In this laboratory you should also be aware of the coming and going of your breath. Neither control nor direct it; simply listen to it, be aware of it. I would say, go knowingly into the process of breathing; go knowingly into the exhalation, which is a natural giving up of all effort. Let the exhalation die in silence, and let the inner need of the body to inhale come up. In this breathing the whole psychosomatic body comes to a very deep relaxation, and there comes a moment when there is a spontaneous giving up of the voluntary process of breathing, and we remain as objectless presence, as objectless awareness. What is important is that we have a glimpse of this objectless presence so that we can later recognize it. It happens very often before the body wakes up in the morning or in the interval between two thoughts or between two perceptions. And it is also in the state of admiration or wonderment or astonishment. Finally, there is a switchover, and one is established in objectless presence in all activities, whether sleeping, eating, thinking or walking. It is a constant meditation. One must be informed of this and keep it in view, or meditation will become a bad habit, and one day you will find you are blocked in your so-called meditation, stuck in a subtle subject-object relationship which you cannot break out of.

Have you anything to say?

I have ideas, prejudices and limitations, and through this veil I listen to what you say. I hear what you say about truth, and the mind accepts it and remembers it in many various and difficult circumstances in life. Is this just a psychological way of escaping from what is really being said, the facts which face me at every moment?

It is necessary that you become completely impregnated on the psychosomatic level with what you have understood. You must become free from patterns, from the past, from all that belongs to non-understanding. Then you will see how you function spontaneously. When you have seen that the "I," the "me," is only a construction in the mind which has no existence in itself, then you give it up, or rather, it gives up itself. It is like an old key which no longer functions in the new door. You ignore it, then you forget it. You forget about being somebody. You no longer have a relation from object to object in your daily life. Being free from the person, you occupy your globality, your totality, your wholeness. Then you become adequate to every situation. Whether you are a lawyer, a religious person, or a doctor, you are appropriate to every moment; you are free from selection, free from choice. You act spontaneously, and your surroundings are stimulated by your way of looking, hearing, acting. You become a truly social person, truly civil, and only then can you help others to be free.

You must live with this understanding. But let us make it clear that you don't *try* to live with your understanding. You can never try to live with your understanding, because you *are* the understanding. You can only see that you don't act according to your understanding.

Where does the desire to meditate come from?

The inner need to meditate comes from deep sleep. It is the experience in deep sleep that brings us to the deep desire to meditate. When the body wakes up in the morning and you say, "I slept well," your body is relaxed, it is true, but "I slept well" really refers to the non-dual experience that you had in deep sleep.

The process of meditation that you described in the beginning, with the senses, with the breathing, is that something we do voluntarily when we want to or when we can?

When a musician wakes up in the morning, he goes spontaneously to his piano and plays. There is no inner intention in it. It is simply for the love of doing it. And a painter in his studio just begins to paint. There is no obligation. Likewise, you should only meditate in your laboratory when you feel drawn to do so. There must be nothing systematic in it. When there is sytematic doing, you become stuck to it, and there is the danger that you will simply be repeating old patterns. When the mind knows that there is something beyond it, it will see that there is nothing more to do, and it will give up. This moment, when you are free from the reflex to be somebody, is the highest opportunity to be still. It is the death of a somebody, of an ego, when there is silence. So if there is anything to be aware of, it is these moments when the mind gives up striving.

There are also moments of pure perception, when there is no naming, no qualification, no interpretation; there is only sense perception. See, also, that you are mostly localized, localized somewhere in your body, localized somewhere in your brain. And you are stuck to the localization. Be aware of it, and bring the seen back to its seeing, consciousness.

How do you do that, bring the seen back to the seeing?

The seen or heard or felt is a deployment of energy. Relax this eccentric energy, and it brings you back to the seeing, hearing, feeling. Then be the seeing; this is consciousness.

This morning you referred to the film and what is before the film. I believe that the identification with the film is the original illness. Could you talk to us about illness and health?

When you are identified with an object, you take away the

57

freedom that the object has. Each object has its own fullness, and it blossoms when allowed to do so. The moment
you become identified with it, the object—in this case the
body—has no more freedom to come to its wholeness, its
health. That is the origin of an unhealthy state. So, in a
certain way, you have given your own answer. Your answer
is right.

*Is it, then, this identification with objects that creates illness,
and does that refer both to gross and subtler objects?*

It belongs to both, to the subtle objects and also to the dense
objects. Object relations create reaction, resistance, defense. But the moment we become aware of our body, then
we find ourselves out of the process. And when we are out
of the process, there is no more complicity.

*Could you talk to us, please, about what is usually called the
subconscious?*

There is only consciousness. There is no unconsciousness
or subconsciousness.

*Must we take it that consciousness is always empty, not
containing anything?*

It is absolutely free from any quality. The only quality is
that it is without any quality.

*You talked about the healing quality of sound. Are you refer-
ring to certain mantras, or something else?*

The right pronunciation of sounds stimulates our organs. The right vibration when pronouncing can stimulate certain organs and heal them. Sounds are very powerful. In America they talk about how smoking pollutes the atmosphere, and it is true. But this pollution, in my opinion, is nothing compared to noise pollution. You can never go anywhere without being obliged to listen to noise, to so-called music.

I am listening carefully to what you say. I do not know English, but I listen to the depth and the sound of what you say, and I feel that sometimes there is communion. When the translation comes, without any fault on the part of the translator, this communion is lost. I believe that words bridge the chasms between situations. But here it seems that the opposite is happening. So, my question is, what are the words, what is the word?

The words are symbols. They are simply the leaves of the rose. But what makes the rose really a rose is its perfume. So I would say, forget the petals and leaves, forget the symbol, and keep the perfume. Don't remember the words. In remembering the words, you go away from the perfume. Forget the words, and keep the perfume. It is only the perfume which makes the word rich. It is also the perfume, the essence, which makes these words your own words. Because, when you live with their perfume, you come to a deeper understanding.

Why do two people get married?

It is a convention which belongs to our society. But marriage is really a sacred happening. You could simply go on the hill at Delphi and get married. You must emphasize the sacredness of marriage. Any other marriage imposed by society is only for security. But to say, "Yes," in a sacred place, that is, for me, a real marriage. In a certain way, marriage should not become an obligation. To be together must be, every day, a sacred function. Otherwise, it is a *plaisanterie*, as they say in French. It belongs to our education and culture that a mother tells her daughter the qualities of a man, and her son the qualities of a woman. The real qualities, not the appearance.

What are these real qualities?

It is somewhat difficult for me to name them. It will be easier for you to name them yourself.

Why do the religions in the world exist?

That is another "why" question. Why?

Is there no answer?

If I were to tell you that I have to leave Delphi tomorrow and I will never be back, would you not have a more important question to ask?

I am thinking of it in the sense that if there were no religions, there would be no wars and humanity would be one.

If you believe it, then keep your belief!

Because I am Jewish, that's it. And we suffered.

Could you talk to us about the limitations that exist in the mind which hinder us from functioning naturally?

We don't need the mind to function in daily life. The function of the mind is thinking. What is thinking? Using symbols. I would say it is a gentlemen's agreement. A symbol is not what is symbolized, and when this is seen the mind stops thinking. The relationship between humans is apparently one of thinking, but there are many other factors which come into a relationship which have nothing to do with thinking. What can you do with your husband or with your boy friend with thinking? Not very much. You are smiling. *Vrai, non?*

Does discipline bring quiet to the mind, or does it destroy it?

A disciplined mind is never a free mind. When you want to become an opera singer, you work your voice and work the music; you learn, and it requires discipline. This discipline is born from the love of singing and music. But you can never learn what you are, because you are profoundly what you are looking for. When you really love something, then you will realize that something and do it spontaneously. Seen from the outside, it may look like discipline, but it is not discipline. When you love something and you inquire into it, you are spontaneously concentrated.

I have a problem on the level of the mind, which sees objects all the time. How can I accept that there are no objects?

But an object which appears in the mind, on the surface of the mind, is only apparently an object. In reality it is an expression of consciousness. I saw the Claude Monet exhibition in London, and when I looked at the objects which appeared on the canvas, they played together, completely absorbed by the light. It is likewise with the supreme light, our light. How can we speak of objects? There is only consciousness, only light. The object is holy when it refers to consciousness.

In our present time, there is a tremendous accumulation of matter, of material things, and we love matter. Is that a hindrance, or how can matter function in a way that it is not a hindrance?

When we make matter function for our use, nothing is wrong. But when we lose the using of the matter and the matter uses us, well, we must stop.

Dr. Klein, I would like you to talk to us about desires, where they come from and how we can deal with them.

The desire in you comes from what you desire. When you give all your intelligence, all your feeling, all your emotion, to your desire, it will take you to what you most desire. Then there comes a reorchestration of all the energies which have been dispersed in your life. And you find yourself, in one moment, in admiring. This reorchestration of your energy, following the explosion of your desire, brings you to an admiring state. You become an admirer. And you can be sure that there comes a fusion of the admirer and the admired, so that there is no longer an admirer and something admired, there is only admiring.

November 6, 1990

Our teaching is essentially based on understanding and what understanding means in the context of truth. Truth here is our real nature, which cannot be objectified. The understanding required to approach truth is thus different from the usual way we understand the world of referents and objects. So the first step is to see the difference between what is understandable—objects—and what is beyond conventional understanding—the objectless.

On the level of the mind, ordinary understanding, the nearest we can come to objectless truth is a clear perspective, a vision of the objectless. I often call this a geometrical representation. The contents of this representation are what could be called the facts of truth: that the mind has limits; that truth is beyond the mind; that truth, our real nature, cannot be objectified, just as the eye cannot see itself seeing; that truth, consciousness, was never born and will never die; that it is the light in which all happenings, all objects, appear and disappear; that in order for there to be understanding of truth, all representation must dissolve. When this representation, the last of the conventional subject-object understanding, dies, it dissolves in its source—the light of which the mind was informed but could not comprehend. In other words, understanding dissolves in *being* understanding. We no longer understand, we are the understanding. This switchover is a sudden, dramatic moment when we are ejected into the timeless.

To say that truth is one is a mental conjecture that calls for objectification. Because we cannot objectify truth, it can only be spoken of in terms of what it is not. As it is beyond subject and object, we call this way non-dual, *advaita*.

Understanding, then, calls for complete openness. When we look from the point of view of the male or female, we only see from the level of gender. When we look from the point of view of the personality, the "I-concept," all is personal, in object-object relationship. But when we take a stand in globality, consciousness, awareness, then there is only consciousness. From the point of view of gender, or the "I-concept," we occupy a mere fraction of being. But when we are in our wholeness, we see only the global. The moment we knowingly occupy our globality, or even have a glimpse of it, the chess board is completely changed. From this point of view, which is no longer a *point* of view, we see things related to one another, because everything now refers to awareness, to silence. All that is phenomenal, all that is objective, only has reality when it abides in, when it refers to, silence, to stillness. So the changing of the chess board is a result of having the forefeeling, or a sudden glimpse, of reality.

Do you have something to say?

Once one is ejected into the timeless, when the geometrical understanding dissolves in being understanding, can one only speak, think, function from the totality? And if so, how can one teach those who do not function in totality?

Only wholeness can teach wholeness. The teacher lives in the totality, and this is itself the teaching.

How then is it possible to teach or relate to those who think from the point of view of time?

As I have often said, the mind cannot change the mind. Only the timeless in me can awaken the timeless in you. The teacher does not refer to the "I," to psychology. It is meaningless to teach at the psychological level about what is beyond the "I."

But surely a certain amount of teaching at the psychological level is helpful.

Helpful for what? Helpful to whom? There are many psychologists in the world but few teachers.

I would like to ask, please, about the role of memory, the function of memory in our lives.

Our memory functions primarily to maintain the "I-concept." We refer very often to the past to create the future and maintain the "I." Up to eighty percent of our waking time is spent in pampering the "I" through day-dreaming. We waste all our energy in day-dreaming. And by day-dreaming I mean all projecting, all strategy, all becoming. Free from the "I-concept," we no longer refer ourselves to the past. So we are free from psychological memory. But

67

when the situation asks for functional memory, practical memory, of course we refer to the past. But this memory is not problematic. It belongs only to the circumstance, to the moment, the situation itself, and dies with the situation.

I would like to ask about the chess board you mentioned. I feel that many times in my life the pieces have merely shifted like a scenario played with small variations. I feel trapped in it. How can I free myself from the trap?

Generally, we function on the level of the male or female, or the "I-concept," and all our relations with our surroundings are from object to object. This is not creative living, it is repetitive. But when we have the forefeeling of what we really are, we are totally open, open to the openness, and the object "I" has no hold. We are openness, the ultimate subject, and we are no longer bound to our surroundings. We are not in our surroundings, but the surroundings are in us. In openness we discover elements in the situation that we never saw before, and we become creative. Then we see things as they are, free from personal interference, free from conflict, free from compulsion. Do you see what I mean?

Does this opening happen from the mind's point of view?

When the mind comes to a moment of helplessness, when the mind says, "I don't know," it means it has come to the end. Then, spontaneously, you are taken by openness. You know moments in life when things come unexpectedly to you and you are not able to refer back, because there is no reference to the past since the situation comes to you so unexpectedly. Then you are obliged to look without thinking, to see facts, to deal with facts. And in facing the situation so, you find yourself in spontaneity. You are the acting, but there is not an actor, there is only acting.

Can I come to know my real nature through art?

Absolutely. Because art is an expression of beauty, of love. Beauty can never be objectified. Beauty is an expression of your totality, of your globality, which, as an artist, you feel as an inner demand to share with the surroundings. You might express it in poetry, in painting, in sculpture, in music or architecture. But it is important to know how to handle the material.

But you are not only an artist when you produce sounds or colors. You are also an artist when, for example, you are looking at art. It is how to look, how to hear, how to touch, how to smell, how to taste, which makes the artist. In true art there is an empty space given by the artist, where the artist, the producer and the observer come together. When both come together, then it is really a beautiful work of art.

Dr. Klein, I have had a taste, I think, of what you are talking about, the stillness, the silence in which there is a kind of choiceless happening. But it seems that there is a connection back to my ego as a kind of insurance policy. My question is, how can I remove that insurance policy and trust fully?

As long as you take yourself for an independent entity, you are bound to the ego. The presence that is silence, stillness, is only in the absence of the person. So it is this deep-rooted idea of being somebody which takes you away from stillness, from silence. Practically speaking, familiarize yourself with listening, looking, hearing, without letting conceptualization interfere. Look, listen, without naming, judging, comparing, evaluating, justifying and so on. Simply live in perception without conceptualization. Because in pure perception there is no room for the person, the "I."

But first be very clear about what you have understood by "I." It is memory, formed by society, belief, information from books and so on. You have identified yourself with this image: "I am this, I am Mr. So-and-so." On the level of the "I-concept" there is no spontaneity, there is only repetition, acting in patterns. In the absence of the "I-concept" there is spontaneity, creativity and invention. In other words, look at things, understand things, without selection. Choice is made by a chooser. Where there is no chooser, there is no choice.

If there is no one who stays open to the perspective of truth, what is it that is open?

It is consciousness which is open, because its nature is only openness. It is completely limitless, because it is not an object. Your real nature is not-knowing. You real nature is timeless. The moment knowing comes in, you create time. There is no weight in openness. The plane offers to carry your luggage in the hold, but sometimes I think you insist on carrying all your luggage yourself!

I think I understand the "I don't know." But, on the other hand, does not the desire to know come from our real nature?

The desire to know comes from what you desire. But what is the motive to know objects, to know situations? Really, objects, whether in functional daily life or in art, are a hallelujah to the ultimate. Every object points to the ultimate, because all the potential in the object is in the ultimate subject. There is no independent object, there is only the autonomous subject. Scientists may believe that there are objects outside us, but after years of understanding, you see that an object only has its reality in the subject. There are not two, there is only one.

What is important is that you are aware that there are spontaneous moments of knowing. When you say, "I understand," the understanding is already depleted, because in this moment you have conceptualized the understanding and made it an object. It is important that the knowing become being knowing, which means that it is completely absorbed in your totality. When this occurs there is a transfer of energy, and your brain, the chess board as we said earlier, changes. You should know that you burn your hands when you say, "I know." Real knowing takes place in your totality. Otherwise, knowing is like collecting stamps.

The first words mentioned this morning were that the teaching has to do with understanding and that the mind must understand what it is not. Could you please talk on this?

The teaching is beyond knowledge. The discriminating mind can only understand what is understandable. The

71

intellectual mind can never know what is beyond knowledge. But when the mind sees this clearly, it relaxes and dissolves into our totality. It then functions as the whole mind or consciousness. As it belongs to this totality, it belongs to reality, to truth, and can have a glimpse of reality. The mind can come to a global geometrical representation of the truth. When the mind is clear, there is no danger that the insight becomes confused in feeling.

You said that when knowing is absorbed in our totality, there is a transfer of energy, and our brain changes. Does this transfer happen suddenly, or is it a gradual process?

The understanding is instantaneous. The switchover from living in the fraction to living the global is also instantaneous. But our body-mind is accustomed to functioning in a fractional way, so it may continue to do so through habit for some time. But there is no longer any impetus in it, and it dies away in totality

This morning on the mountain, watching the beauty in front of me, opening, hearing the sounds and seeing everything, I became aware that there were two: me looking at the beauty. When I saw this, it seemed as though I wasn't really seeing or hearing, and I didn't really know what was in front of me, and I felt completely lost. This is an observation. There is no question.

In looking there is no looker, there is only looking. There is no "observer" and no "observed." An observed is only possible when there is an observer, but the observer is a creation of the mind. See that in looking at the mountains there is only looking. In any case, you are present. But a moment later your mind creates a witness. So eliminate the observer, and the observed automatically disappears too. Looking is then oneness; consciousness is one with its so-called object.

When you look at the mountains, your five senses must be open. You taste, smell, feel, touch, hear the mountain. You are in total receptivity. Because—and I know you can't say this in the Greek language—the seen is in the seeing, what you look at has its potentiality, its reality, in you as the ultimate looker.

When we speak of being open, we must be completely open. This is very important. The looking, the hearing, the listening, must become organic. By organic I mean that the body, the five senses, must be included. For example, when you look at this beautiful valley here and you go really into the valley with your tactile sensation, your body sensation, you feel yourself without any boundaries. Then there is a feeling of freedom which brings great joy. Or when you are in front of a big green meadow and you go into every corner of the green, you bathe in the green, then you come out feeling completely fresh, because green has a very strong power, the power to emphasize existence, to make you feel more integrated, more alive.

Similarly, when you look at a beautiful stone, you may feel the quality of the stone, its stone-stillness. It lives in its stillness. The reason for its existence is its stillness. And so when you really go into the stone and feel its heaviness and follow all the variations of its form, its cavities and convexity, it brings you to stillness. Really looking at a stone, being one with it, makes you also still.

It sounds, from what you say, as though the senses are, in one way, the organs of knowledge and as if, through the senses, the qualities of things go into our essential nature.

Yes, when the object is received by the senses, it is a pure perception not captured by the mind. Only in pure perception free from any mental qualification can an object give its secret to us completely. The perceived dissolves in perceiving.

And this is the secret, to bring us back to the perceiving?

Absolutely. The perceiving is our real nature, consciousness, the homeground of all objects.

Can we have a break for a few minutes?

———

When we say that we must come to the end of the mind, that we must exhaust the mind, is it a necessary process, something which must happen, or is it possible to have an insight without the mind being exhausted? And secondly, is this process itself a meditation, or does meditation begin at the end of the mind?

When the mind goes to its end—and it goes to its end when it thinks of the unthinkable—we can call it meditation, because in thinking the unthinkable, we are silent. Our thinking no longer starts from thinking, it starts from silence. When the mind comes to the end of its potentiality, it is a relaxed mind. This means that when there is something to think, it thinks, and the rest of the time it is in non-thinking, that is, a natural state of relaxed, non-directed attention. If we do not come to the end of the thinking mind, we will be bound to it, so that even when there are moments when there is nothing to think, we are still in the mind and live in constant agitation. The relaxed mind functions in discontinuity. Only when it functions like this can we be aware of the continuity behind all functioning. The continuity is timeless meditation. It is this presence which gives life and reality to all appearings. Any other so-called meditation you might do has no flavor. But really, meditation is praying, praying without someone who prays or is prayed to. Real praying is thanking for the joy of being. It is expressed at every moment. Experiences like joy, transcendence, peace and holiness, are all expressions borrowed from the mind. But the meditation we are talking about here is without any qualification. Its only quality is that it is without qualifications. It is the extinction of everything that could be a state.

As long as the mind is not exhausted, it will still be an obstacle to any real insight. Because the uninformed mind, that is, the mind which does not know its limits, will continue to try to understand what is beyond it. It will be driven by will or unconscious reflex, in the old patterns of becoming and attaining. The mind will still be looking for freedom, but in trying to attain it, it goes further away from it. Because there is no way to go to freedom, for there is nobody to go to it. When the mind remains in the reflex that there is something to attain, something to become, something to achieve, it cannot come to the only useful perspective for the mind, the perspective of living in not-knowing. When the mind abides in not-knowing, when it is, at every moment, open to the unknown, it is a tool of higher reasoning. Any other use of the mind is a nuisance.

The important thing is to realize that what we are looking for is the looker, is our presence. To achieve something in the phenomenal realm we must, of course, refer to something we already know. But regarding that which can never be an object, we must go away from it. We must come to the organic memory of the body. This is important, because through this organic memory we will come to the absolutely relaxed state, where we have all our energy in our hand, so to speak. In this relaxed state the body and the mind come more or less together. There is no more duality. As we have said before, the relaxed body is dynamic, not passive. Passive relaxation is still in duality. It is not integrated because there is still emphasis on the object, relaxation.

Even in a relaxed state, the mind automatically creates pictures, or thoughts. How can we exhaust the mind?

These are residues, and these residues must also come to their exhaustion. When we let them come to their exhaustion, we have a forefeeling of the "I am." Don't go into the images or thoughts of these residues. Some teachers say to observe them, listen to them, but don't go in, don't follow them. My experience is that we must not observe or listen or follow them, because the moment we look at them we feed them by creating a witness to them. Take your stand in the void, the "I am." From here, you ignore them. But I

76

think that when you become aware of the body, not the concept body but the feeling body, and you are at one with the feeling, in this becoming aware of the true body feeling, the residues of images and words and language have no more power. You are, of course, still in subject-object relation, the perceiver and the perceived body feeling, but there comes a moment where there is only the "I am."

When we are living in our tactile, global body, we are no longer in our foreheads. Generally, we live in our foreheads, and this localization prevents all global sensation. When we remain in our foreheads, we are in the hands of the devil. So we must become free from the brain. In the beginning there may be some difficulty to be free from the brain, because it is partly activated by the the taking and grasping of the eyes, which are very connected with the brain. It is important, therefore, to consciously relax the eyes, to sense the hollows of our eyes, their heaviness. When this part is sensitive, there is a deep relaxation in the brain. Some scientists don't believe we can sense our brain, but they are studying medicine in a superficial way. We can sense and change our brain. For when the brain becomes relaxed, we feel ourselves no longer localized in the thinking factory of the forehead, but we feel ourselves behind, in the upper cervical vertebrae. When we feel ourselves behind, in our neck, we can no longer see from the point of view of the individual which projects individual objects. Because the individual is a thought construct which comes from the frontal area. From behind there is no longer any concretization. There is only a vague cloud of objectivity. Then this subtle localization behind in the neck dissolves down into the heart, and the heart is the last door, the last expansion. Finally, we become free also from the heart. We become emptiness, emptiness without border and without center. We are the universe and the universe is us.

But I would say, take note of all this and immediately forget it.

November 7, 1990

There are times when I feel a certain laziness and have feelings of guilt because of this laziness. Can you talk about it, and whether there is a way to face it?

When you feel lazy, face your laziness on the level of the body. This calls for a fresh attention, an attention free from expectation. When your acting starts from thinking, there can be no creativity. But when it starts from silence, there is creativity. So become free from memory. Listen with innocence to your laziness. You will see that listening is an art. When you listen to your body, free from memory, from the past—in other words, free from volition—there is no longer any accomplice to the laziness. There is no repetition; every moment in life is new. Your body is new at every moment, because it is created at every moment. There are so many different levels to the body, so many different ways of sensing the body. This palette is at your disposal when you are free from the conditioned body.

As I listen, I am observing the state of my body, and I notice that there is a certain tension in the back and between the eyebrows, which is a hindrance to real listening. Could you please talk about the tension in the body?

79

Tensions are reactions. That means that you have established a personal relationship with certain circumstances. When you react, there is a localization of certain energies, especially within the eye region. Try, in daily life, not to look at things, but to let things look at you. In this way you will free yourself from grasping, from taking.

With the help of your imagination, let your eyes drop completely down out of their cavities. Feel them suspended in front of you. See how this visualization acts on you, on your brain.

There should be a global feeling of your body, but you will discover that you have sensation only in certain fractions. In the evening before the body falls asleep and in the morning before the body wakes up, you should have the global feeling of your body. Let it become an object of observation, an observation that is completely free from expectation or anticipation, that is not directed. It is simply observing, completely innocent, like the observing of a child. When the body is relaxed, all the sense organs are receptive. Then, instead of grasping an object, you let it come to you, you feel it crossing your eyes, your brain. I would say that when the object comes to you, when the energy crosses your eyes, it is a very deep feeling of softness, of love, a feeling of healing.

How important is it to practice this relaxing of the observation? Is it something we should do every moment we can let go of the jumping reflex?

Yes! Until it becomes your own; until the reflex is eliminated.

Dr. Klein, I would like to ask about the relationship between the teacher and the disciple. How does the student find the teacher, and is there a difference in the relation between the disciple and his special teacher or can the disciple have many advisors? How can the disciple be sure that his teacher is his teacher?

The self is looking for the Self. When the Self is looking for itself, that is the highest teaching. In other words, there is a moment when the teacher finds you. You are pushed by the presence of the teacher into your real objective nature. The relationship between teacher and disciple is quite magical. The teacher never takes you for an ignorant person, never takes you for a disciple, because he does not take himself for a teacher. To take oneself for a teacher is a restriction, and to take yourself for an ignorant person, a disciple, is a restriction. The moment you become free from this restriction there is a current, a current of oneness.

Regarding your other question—how can you be sure you have found the one who can help you, help you realize what you profoundly are—you must never feel bound to the teacher. You should feel yourself really free from the teacher, because the teaching is that you become free, free from yourself, from what you are not. To feel yourself, in the highest sense, absolutely free, you must not be bound to anything, or anyone, or any institution. I think you understand what I mean. It is quite simple. Being free is freedom from everything. Affection never binds you. In affection there is freedom. The relationship doesn't exclude affection.

I would like to ask you again about discipline, this time in relation to children. What form should discipline for the child take?

A child should be brought up absolutely freely, but in this freedom there should be a certain rhythm, a rhythm of sleeping, of eating, of working. When the child loves something, he will do it spontaneously, with a natural concentration. There should be no obligation. When you love something, spontaneously there is discipline, there is one-pointedness. There is no need to force discipline and concentration. When you do this, you live in end-gaining; you project a goal, a result, so you are not open to the unexpected. Show the child how to look, how to listen, etc., not what to look at or what to listen to. A child must learn how to explore.

Can you give me a concrete example of showing a child how to look, not what to look at? For example, if we take the child to an aquarium, how would you proceed?

Stimulate the child to look in all ways, to see the relation of one fish to another, the light, color, water, how the movement of the fish is unexpected, and so on.

But this is saying what to look at.

Yes. But not in the conventional way: "There's a fish".

I would like to ask about dreams. What are dreams, and do they have a prophetic quality?

Certain dreams have a prophetic quality, but, generally, dreams are residues from the waking state which need elimination. But when there is a so-called prophetic dream, don't remain stuck to the object, to the image. Rather, see how the image has acted on you. See how you feel when you come out of the dream. Certainly don't try immediately to interpret it. Let the feeling be feeling.

Essentially, there is no great difference between the waking state and the dreaming state. In the dreaming state you bite an apple and taste the sweetness the same as in the waking state. It is only when you are in the waking state that you say the dream was a mental production. But as long as the dreamer belongs to the dream, the so-called waking state is also a dreaming state.

What is laughter? It seems that the moment we laugh, we are in a different situation from that in which we are usually.

Laughing is an expression of the heart. It is not, as Freud would have it, a sexual reaction. When there is laughing, nobody laughs, there is only laughing. In laughing, the object of your laugh is completely dissolved. Perhaps one could say that after the absolute understanding, we laugh.

What is the function of the mind? In other words, why was it given to man?

All is mind.

Isn't everything consciousness?

Mind, like everything else, appears in consciousness. The mind is an organ, a tool. It has a purely functional character. But we should be clear about what we call mind. In certain traditions one speaks of the whole mind, and one takes the whole mind to be consciousness. Consciousness is not separate from mind; mind appears in consciousness. All the phenomenal world is mind.

Moments of pure observation are only moments, because the mind comes in immediately, almost like a muscular reaction, to reestablish the previous state. I would like to know if there is a way that these moments of pure observation can be made longer.

In pure observation, which happens when the concept doesn't come in, there is no place for an "I-image." Conceptualization is a reflex of the "I-image." Accustom yourself to pure observation without any intervention.

It is normal that when you observe something, you name it. This belongs to your culture. Naming, language, is a normal brain function. But the moment you qualify it, you use memory, and when this happens there is no longer pure observation. See those mechanical reflexes, but do not try to change them. Rather, try to hear, to look, to touch, like the poet, without qualification. A real poet, like any artist, lets the object completely unfold. He remains in pure perception, because the pure perception is very rich. Generally, through wrong habit, we focus first on the thing, the object. But the real way to behave is first to become aware of the space. Don't grasp the tree immediately with your senses, usually the eyes. Feel the space around the tree.

When you feel the space, it is a tactile sensation, on the level of body feeling. Your body occupies all the space, which includes you, the tree and all your surroundings. Then the object appears in the space. Likewise, take note how it is light which makes an object an object. Look how the light caresses the object. Be aware of the dark and the light in the object. An object does not exist in isolation. It is always in relation with other objects. See the relation between the different objects, and so on. There are so many things to say about this, but in the end it is your feeling which is necessary for exploration. An object needs awareness to be known. It needs your own light to be an object. All this belongs to pure observation. The "I" has no place here; it doesn't come in.

So are you saying that, in pure observation, the senses function, but not the thinking process?

Only the senses, yes.

So the way to sustain the absence of the ego reflex is to let the senses explore the object, and not the mind?

Yes.

It is the thinking mind which restricts the pure perceiving.

Yes.

So the only function of the mind is the cognition that it is a tree and not an elephant. That's very quick, and then that's all.

Absolutely.

In awareness, what determines which sense is active at which instant?

Someone who has no sense of smell may first see the rose. A painter may first see the rose, then smell it. Someone else may first be attracted to the texture. It depends on the make-up, the inner need or condition, of the individual. It seems as if there is simultaneity of all the senses, but this is not so. The mind gives us the impression of simultaneity. In reality, consciousness is one with its object.

When we look, feel and hear, and all our sense perceptions come into play, then we really explore the world with our global body including the energy body. When we look at a valley with our tactile sensation, it leaves us free from all impediment, it makes us free from all frontiers. We feel the body expanded in space.

I'm sorry, I'm not sure that I understood correctly.

When you look at the valley with your sense perceptions, with your tactile sensation, you are no longer here, you are in the valley. This expansive state acts on your body; you feel free from any borders. The "I-concept" is a contraction and looks for security, for survival in fixed situations. But in the expanded light body, there is no room for the "I-concept." In looking one must be free from the looker.

You have often mentioned the opening, or openness. Would you please talk about this?

When you are free from memory, you are open to every situation. When you are free from end-gaining, free from striving, free from expectation, then you are open, open to all the possible facts. Otherwise, you are only open to the past, and that means to repetition. When you are open to all the facts, there is no repetition. Every moment is new. Life is never repetitious. It is because of our way of looking and acting from the "I-concept" that there appears to be repetition. Because we superimpose old ideas on the situation, we are not open to the newness, open to the unknown. We must be open to the unknown. This openness with your surroundings is harmonious living. In openness there is love.

Begin with your body, your nearest surroundings. Generally, when the body wakes up in the morning, it is the pattern in your mind which you think is your body, which wakes up. Free yourself from the pattern; see that it is a pattern. Let the feeling of your body wake up, not the pattern. Then you will see that it is the same with your surroundings, your children, your wife, your husband, your neighbor and so on. You have been living with them as you live with furniture, because you superimpose patterns on your surroundings. It is very tragic when you come to middle age and see that you have contacted all your surroundings through an image. It happens with couples who have been together a long time. People talk too much and observe too little.

I have noticed that often there is a holding back of feeling, and that creates a problem even in the breathing. Does that have to do with opening?

87

Yes. When you approach the breathing, first emphasize the exhalation. The exhalation is a giving up, a letting go, in all parts of your body. Feel where there is a block in this giving up, where the exhalation cannot reach. When the exhalation is completely accomplished, you will discover a new inhalation, because all the residues will be given up during the exhalation and the inhalation will be much more profound. If you do not let the exhalation come completely to the end, then you repeat your reactions, your conditioning. The old body patterns are reaffirmed with every inhalation. With the full exhalation you let go of your conditioning, you free yourself.

In the beginning just listen to the natural flow of inhalation and exhalation. Feel where the natural breathing is localized. Is it on the upper part of the tongue, or the lower part, or the center? Is it in the abdominal region or cervical region? When you exhale, let the exhalation die completely with all its residues. It should be a total giving up, but you will see what doesn't give up. You keep something within you. It takes time to explore this faculty, your exhalation. You must exert yourself in a certain way, not by repetition but in observing.

In the end you will feel how the exhalation and the inhalation are superimpositions on silence, on stillness. When the exhalation is completely accomplished, there is an interval of non-activity. One should be completely attuned to this moment of silence. And then let the body take its own departure for the inhalation. At every moment there is the white sheet. When you feel the white sheet after the exhalation and before the inhalation, you will soon feel it after the inhalation and before the exhalation. Then you

88

will be aware that exhalation and inhalation appear on the white sheet. Exhalation and inhalation appear, but the white sheet always is.

Yesterday you talked about a certain procedure to be "behind," passing across the eyes, the forehead, the neck, the heart, and then to emptiness. Could you please talk more about this? Is this explanation meant as a kind of practice which could be done every day? Can you also elaborate on emptiness?

It is a fact that all the elaborations of thinking are more or less in the factory which is situated in the forehead. This causes tension, and this tension is very related to eyesight. Practically speaking, therefore, one should come to a very deep relaxation of the eyes. In doing so, there's the sensation that both eyebrows are very heavy. You come to relaxation with the impression that the left and right eyebrows are two curtains which fall down over your face. Then feel the left side of the brain, if there is tension, contraction, or a slight vibration. Also the right brain. At first you will not be able to sense your brain. But if you make it feeling, you can, with this feeling, empty the brain of tension. Then go with the feeling, down behind in the direction of the neck, in the direction of the old brain.

It is very difficult to remember all this without actually doing it. Will you guide us through it later today?

This evening we will have the opportunity to do it. We are mainly localized in our head. Even when there is nothing to think, there is a habitual localization in the forehead.

When you are localized in your neck instead of your forehead, the energy which comes up from the lower part of your spinal cord to strike the brain is stopped in a certain way in the cervical region, before it can become a concrete thought. It remains in its potentiality without direction or volition. This last localization gives way to expansion in the heart. The energy is completely free, not localized anywhere. You feel yourself completely expanded. The heart is the last threshold. Abide in the heart.

With the help of this exercise, you occupy your global being, where there is no periphery and no center and you can come to a glimpse of what you fundamentally are, but can never objectify.

I know you will say this is second-hand information, but in the texts it says that the energy flows up the spine into the crown chakra and out of the top of the head. But you say that when the energy is localized in the cervical region, it then drops down into the heart, and this is the last threshold. Why is there such an apparent discrepancy between the texts I have read and your words? And is there a time when the energy explodes in the head instead of the heart?

What I say comes from experience. What you say comes from books. The crown chakra is a stage in Yoga. It has nothing to do with the direct way.

Dr. Klein, would you please talk about feelings and the expression of feelings? For example, should feelings always be allowed to be expressed?

We could speak of two categories of feelings: what we call affectivity or emotivity, which is a state, a defense, a reaction, where we have established a personal relationship with our surroundings; and emotion, which is an expression, I would say, of the heart. This expression must be offered without any restriction. But we should become aware of affectivity, which is a reaction of the ego mind. See very clearly what is emotivity and what is emotion.

Thank you for listening.

November 8, 1990

Let your mind be very clear that when you are looking for
your real self, it is it which is looking for itself. That is why
you can never find it—because it is the ultimate looker
which looks for itself. In other words, you are fundamentally already what you are. Any movement you undertake
is a going away from it. You sit on this chair and you cannot
find yourself on the chair by going somewhere else. So the
inevitable question is, "How can I become aware of what I
am?" But we cannot be aware of the "I am." We can only
be aware of things. All that we are aware *of* is an object, but
what we already are, our real nature, is not an object. It is
consciousness, the light behind all objects. It is the ultimate
perceiver in which the perceived appears and disappears. It
is its own perceiving. So it can never be understood in terms
of subject-object relationship. The perceiver can never be
perceived, as the eye cannot see its seeing.

All that is perceived, you are not. When you understand
this, you are no longer concerned with what you are not,
and there is a natural giving up of what you are not. All the
energy that was eccentric, spent in achieving, becoming,
grasping and so on, comes to a stop. And there is only
stillness, silence, which is the original perception of the real
self. It is your globality. In this globality, there is not a

knower of the globality; otherwise, it could not be globality. We can only say, as in all the sacred sayings, it knows itself by itself.

Are there any questions?

Apart from coming together like this, what can help us in this understanding?

Let yourself become completely impregnated by these sayings. Take note of what we are saying here. You can only take note of it when you are open to it, ready for it, ready to be aware of it. By impregnated I mean our whole psychosomatic body should be in this taking note. Be completely impregnated with the essence of this taking note. Take only the oil from the olives. Let go of all that is not the pure oil. The moment we see, we hear, we realize that the looker is what he is looking for, it causes a revolution in us. It brings us back to ourselves. It frees us from all objects.

Dr. Klein, you said that we must be open to it, be ready for it. Often it happens that one doesn't know if one is open or ready.

You are ready when you have the full desire to actualize it. Then you are ready.

It seems that if life brings me to such a crisis point I may be fortunate, but so far I have counted myself lucky that it hasn't! What can I do to come to the not-knowing state if I am not forced there by a real crisis?

The self is always there, asking for actualization. It is

sometimes concealed by the phenomenal world and the asking does not appear strongly. But it appears.

The mind knows that in its absence there is presence, so it is open to giving up, ready to give up. You think there is something to attain and you are in a state of volition. In a state of volition there is anticipation. You are too preoccupied with your projection. It touches you on the shoulder, but you don't feel it.

Let us have a break for ten minutes.

Why are some people here and not others? Why is my mother here and not my sister?

Why not ask your sister? This is first and foremost a friendly meeting. A friendly meeting is a meeting in love. And I suppose that there is earnestness in this meeting, the earnestness to really look and explore what is life. The fact that you are earnest means that you have already looked in many directions. The desire to look in many directions to find life, your real being, comes from an inner urge to know truth, the inner urge to find yourself. When you look very seriously in every direction, you become exhausted and are left in a state of psychological bankruptcy. You feel utterly helpless; you are in despair; you no longer know where to turn; every avenue leads to a dead end; your mind can no longer help you. This crisis is the most important point in your life. You are left in a state of complete not-knowing. You have no hopes or expectations. It is a rare opportunity where the mind is faced with its limits and, being of no further use, it abdicates, gives itself up. Then you are open, open to nothing, open only to the openness. This openness is the threshold of your real nature. Abide there in not-knowing and you will see what happens.

I would like to ask about feelings of guilt and remorse, and whether observation of these feelings helps them to dissolve.

Guilt is guilt for whom? First ask yourself this. But don't wait for an answer. Live in the question. The one who feels guilty is only a thought-construct. He has no autonomous being. So live knowingly in the question and all is forgiven!

Why is it that sometimes I even feel pleased when something negative happens to another? It seems a very bad trait!

It is the "I-image" which feels "I am safe," because it looks for security in every circumstance. Be aware when this complacent feeling comes up that it comes up from the "I," the "me." You should have a non-objective relationship with yourself and with others. It is the only way to become free from this reflex. Feel the light and be the light in every circumstance, and you will not be solicited by habits and reflexes.

I am visited very often by states which create a constant conflict in me. They feel like residues from many situations which I did not face in the moment itself. What shall I do about it?

There is not one look for each state. There is one look for all states. When you live in selection, you live in conflict.

It is only on the level of the mind that there are negative and positive feelings. The mind functions in duality. Positive and negative for whom? It is a concept. On the level of the mind you remain in a vicious circle of positive and negative. But when you see it, you are beyond complementarity. You can never become aware of something unless you are outside of the process of which you are aware. But then be it. Don't involve yourself any more with positive and negative, but be the seeing. This seeing is not a concept, it is an inner light. It is the light which sees. You see, it needs a very deep intimacy with one's self.

In everyday life we meet each other, and really what meets is the personality. How can one come to the point where it is not a personality meeting a personality?

See, in the moment itself, the deep reflex to take yourself for somebody—for example, to take yourself as the someone's wife, but you are not only a wife. When you take yourself for a wife, you are bound, stuck to the wife, and there can only be a relationship between a wife and a husband. That is object-object relationship. Free yourself from being a wife, and, in your totality, you will be love. Then your so-called husband is no longer your husband, but is also changed, not from the point of the wife, but through love. When you take yourself for a wife, you see only a husband. When the husband takes himself for a husband, he sees only a wife. I do not deny that in certain circumstances the so-called husband asks for a wife, and the so-called wife asks for a husband. But to be bound to this relationship, object to object, man to woman, personality to personality, is to live in rules, in patterns. There is no more life in it. It becomes boring. Sometimes you feel bound, and you change one pattern for another, one wife for another. But there is still no real spontaneity, no love. When we see clearly how we function, how we contact our surroundings through memory from the point of view of separate roles and patterns, the already known, we can only be astonished. In this object-object relationship there is not enough exploration. There is no inquiry, because the ego, the person, doesn't like to inquire, since inquiring calls for being free from the person. Inquiry is the death of the person. When you live without roles, in the non-relationship, there is constantly something new. Even on the sexual level, there is freshness. Otherwise, it is just a reflex, and that is the death of the relationship. I do not very much like the word sexuality. Let us call it love relation: looking in the eyes, a touch of the hand, a brush of the shoulder—that is, for me, love-making.

To continue this question of the relation between man and woman, what is to be done with the roles that have been assigned to us by society, that the husband's role is to work, to earn money, and the wife's role is to stay at home, raise children and obey the husband? Is there any meaning in following these roles?

One cannot codify behavior. When behavior is codified, there is no life in it. If you like being at home, arranging flowers and reading the poems of Rilke to your husband when he comes home, then that is very beautiful; do it. But don't do it as a role.

And if you don't like doing that? (everyone laughs)

Then do something you do like.

So do you ignore the society?

You are in the society, but you are not of the society. It is necessary to have certain rules for children and for the immature. Otherwise, the society would be in chaos. But when one imposes these rules, it must be with the background knowledge that it is only for a period of time until we are aware and free from ourselves. But when a so-called husband and wife live together, they should be free from rules. There is a time for codified morality, but this has nothing to do with living your freedom. When you are free from yourself, you spontaneously act morally.

There is authority, but there is no one who is authoritative.

I would like to ask about fear. I am not talking about fear in the abstract, but about certain situations when the conditions are such that you are afraid that someone is going to harm you. For example, I am afraid to stay alone in a place that I don't know well. I have seen this fear, I have tried to understand it, but it's so strong that I can't do anything about it.

It is the memory of a situation in the past.

Isn't there also biological survival? For example, you would never recommend that a woman walk down a dark road at night alone. You yourself are quite protective in these matters.

It is true that biological survival comes in.

That's what I wanted to ask about.

Try to arrange your life so that you are never in a situation where you have to defend yourself. But, in your case, the fear comes from memory, from a past experience.

At the beginning of this morning's talk you were talking about stillness, which is, you said, your nearest, your very being, this fundamental stillness. Most of the time one sees a great deal of activity in the mind, and there is a belief, at least in the progressive approach, that one needs to still the mind before one can come to the fundamental stillness. But is it true that the mind could be very active with lots of thoughts, and one could be in this fundamental stillness? It must be so, because the fundamental stillness is there all the time. So the question is: how does one contact this fundamental stillness even while the mind is thinking or while there is activity in the mind?

A quiet mind is the result of a profound conviction that there is nothing to achieve. Because then the mind relaxes and is used only as a tool for facing situations in the environment. As long as you still think or act as though there is something to attain, the mind is in constant move-ment. So the mind must understand that consciousness is beyond it. Then it gives up. This giving up comes only through understanding. You cannot make your mind still. It becomes quiet as the result of understanding.

I think my question is, if one is not the mind, it does not really matter whether it is still or not. Or does it?

A still mind, I mean a mind which knows its limits, is open to everything. Only in a mind which knows its limits are there windows, windows through which the light of consciousness enters. In the confused mind there is no light of reality. It is only through a deep understanding that the mind becomes still. And this deep understanding calls for a mind which is completely open, not looking, not desiring, not grasping.

Do you mean still, not moving, or still, without agitation?

One must make the distinction between functional moving and agitation. The nature of the mind is function. It functions according to situations in daily life. But the mind which does not know its limits is agitated, looking constantly to be something.

Please, I feel closed in in every way. My mind has no windows, and I don't understand why I exist.

You are life where there is no one who lives. If you take yourself for a liver, it interrupts life. If you take yourself for someone who lives, you are bound to this someone. Be open to life, because in your natural state you are open. There is not one who is open. You are simply openness itself.

Mozart composed many operas, Shakespeare wrote many plays, Napoleon won many wars. But nobody wrote music, no one wrote a play, no one won a war. They are only happenings. Many books have been written, but nobody has written them.

You said that we must let objects come to us, and not go to objects. Would you talk more about that, please?

Before you think, before you name, there is silence. Before the watch goes tick, before the watch goes tock, there is space. When the object dissolves in silence, there is only silence. All that is perceived appears and disappears in silence. Its homeground is silence, is stillness, awareness, consciousness. When an object is not seen in the homeground to which it belongs, it is an object with no meaning. An object becomes sacred, becomes truth, when it refers back to its homeground.

When you live in your globality, all the senses function without grasping, in expansion. They welcome surroundings. The brain is also a sense organ, and when it is relaxed it simply recognizes the object and welcomes the information from the senses. But our body and mind are rarely in this relaxed, receptive state. The senses are contracted and grasp. The brain qualifies, judges, compares, thinks about, and analyzes the object. All this brain activity is around the ego, memory. Stay with the pure perception before the mind comes in.

So you distinguish between naming and qualifying?

Yes. Naming is a function of, and reflects, the brain in your culture. When you name something, it is only to make it clear that the book is not a pen. But when you begin to qualify it, to interpret it, then you are in the mind, then you make it psychological.

But it happens awfully fast.

Yes. But become aware of it and postpone the qualification and remain longer in pure perception. We should look at objects the way an artist does. The name appears in order to tell us it's a tree and not a snake; then it dissolves and we are left in pure perception without any qualification. In this way the creative expression is not limited. You can see when a painter has remained in the name because the painting is lifeless. But whereas for the artist, the object, the world, is sense perception, the truth seeker goes one step further and sees that the sense perception is grounded in the totality which is consciousness.

Why do people not understand the unity of happiness and remain separate?

As objects they are separate, but as ultimate subjects they are not separate, they are one. But the first thing is that you wake up in what you are fundamentally. Don't try to think it, because it is unthinkable. Your questions begin very often with why. Free yourself from the why. The why keeps you in your mind.

How can I listen to the words of truth?

You can only understand truth by truth. When you listen free from all anticipation or expectation, then you are open. You should follow the sayings and be one with them without letting the qualifying mind come in. This brings you to the perspective, the right orientation. It is only in living with this understanding that you come to the feeling of the essence. And there is a moment when there is a giving up of the understanding which belongs to the mind and what remains is only the oil from the olive, the essence. We use words as symbols, but the symbols are not what they symbolize. Your question is heard in silence, and the answer comes out of silence. Only this speaking has pedagogical value; otherwise, it is only just talking. So don't be stuck to the words.

If the understanding of our real nature were to take place, would it not happen in the first moment that one comes in contact with a true teacher? If so, it seems that what we call the spiritual search is a pleasant, mental game. But, as you mentioned already, Dr. Klein, there is a certain pedagogical value in meetings like this. What is it that suddenly will change the situation, so that there will be understanding?

When you see that what you thought was a snake is actually a rope, what happens? You saw a snake in your garden and were afraid. Is the snake faster than you? Then suddenly, you see it is a rope, and what happens in you? You are not only aware of a change in the situation outside, but you are aware of the inside. You see your imagination, all your fear, all your tension, and how they suddenly dissolve. When you see truth, something happens in you. You become aware of the untruth. And then you go back and see that what you took for untruth is also truth. It is only understanding that brings the change of energy, a reorchestration of all the energy that was dispersed. The insight must strike the body-mind; otherwise, it is only intellectual play.

Can you talk about painting?

First, the painter must disappear, so that there is only painting. Why paint nature? Nature is already perfect. Why copy something which is already perfect? In this case, painting is a nuisance. When there is a real understanding of the perfection of nature, this perfection brings you to transpose the perfection. Only in this transposition of the perfection of nature is there any meaning in painting it. In transposing it, you exalt certain points of this perfection. This is all you can do, excite certain parts, certain aspects. Don't copy nature, learn how to transpose it.

When you spoke before of the example of the snake and the rope, I think I heard it in two ways. The first way was the distinction between illusion and truth, and the second way was that, seen from truth, one could see the object as either a snake or a rope, and it wouldn't matter, as both are equally objects. Was I hearing correctly?

When you see what you think is a snake, it has a strange impact on you. Your mind may think of many possibilities: "It may be poisonous; I may have to go to the hospital," etc. You have established a personal relationship with the object based on biological survival and memory, and fears may come up. Then you see that it is a rope. This is the traditional teaching. But what you say is right, because, from the ultimate point of view, both are objects. The rope does not have such a strong impact on me, but my relationship with it is still one of subject-object. Actually, both are objects appearing in mind. You can never speak of a fact when you establish a personal relationship with the object.

You sometimes speak of the object revealing itself in its fullness. When this happens, is there a dimensional quality that appears, a dynamism so that it no longer appears fixed or static?

In any case, an object is not static. It is memory that makes it static. When you see an object free from memory, it presents itself from many angles, in many forms, in many lights. But it is your own light consciousness in which all of this takes place.

I ask because I have had the experience of looking at an object and just looking without controlling it, letting it flow. And it became dynamic, colorful, and all around it was shimmering. Was this a pure perception?

No. It is your own imagination which you projected. You are still looking for an experience. William Blake saw many things, even many angels! It has nothing to do with seeing things as facts.

How can an object point to my real nature?

The seen has its potentiality in the seeing, in other words, in consciousness. It appears in consciousness, and it disappears in consciousness. When you realize that the seer can never be seen, as the eye can never see its seeing, then there comes a stop. That the looker is what he is looking for is the final understanding. Because, otherwise, all you can find are objects. The essential understanding is that there is no understander and nothing to understand, there is only understanding. Be the understanding.

November 9, 1990

Feel your feet in contact with the ground. Feel yourself erect, straight, vertical. Move your neck slightly back, so you feel that the cervical region is a prolongation of the rest of your spinal cord. Be aware of the position of your shoulders and shoulder blades. The slightest rising up of the shoulders is a defense. Feel your nostrils. Feel the entrance to your nostrils. Feel the coming and going of the breath several inches in front of the entrance to the nostrils. Do not control the breath or have any pretension of being an observer. Feel the expansion of the breath in the upper part of your torso, on the level of your collarbones. Be completely one with the coming and going of the breath, which is localized on the level of the collarbones. Then feel the expansion of the breath a little lower, in the center, the middle part of your trunk. Now completely ignore the upper part. Be one with the coming and going of the breath. Then feel the expanding of the breath in the lower part, the abdominal region. Ignoring the upper and middle regions, go knowingly into the process. Then inhale with all of the regions: lower, middle, upper part; exhale upper part, middle part, lower part. The inhalation and the exhalation take place exclusively through the nostrils.

Let the exhalation go completely to the end. Sometimes

you think that you are at the end, but there is still some residue. So go to the very end of the exhalation, but without forcing the air out. Then be completely attuned to the silence after the exhalation, and wait for the inner need of the body to inhale. Feel the exhalation and inhalation several inches in front of the nostrils. There must be no intention in the frontal region of the brain. It then is completely relaxed. There is no rising up of the shoulders. Keep them down, knowingly. There are no gaps or stops and starts in the inhalation and the exhalation; it is one steady flow, from beginning to end, the same intensity. You live from moment to moment; there is no anticipation to an end. You follow from moment to moment. Be aware during the inhalation that it is not a grasping, a taking. And let the exhalation completely die in silence. There is a moment when there is a forgetting of the inhalation and exhalation, and awareness is in identity with the silence between exhalation and inhalation. Be this identity with the silence.

There is no grasping in the inhalation and no pushing in the exhalation. Feel the space in front of you. Go completely into the space. You have the impression that the pause between the exhalation and inhalation is in this space, in this prolongation of your body. With this space feeling in front of you, open the left wing of your body. Feel the space in the left side simultaneously with the front. Go to the right wing. Feel the space there. And now your body is completely expanded in front, on the left and right. Try to touch the space with your tactile sensation. Now visualize the space behind you. Go completely in the space behind you and let the exhalation and inhalation be in this space

110

behind you. Now give up visualizing in front, behind, left and right, because you can never visualize it all simultaneously. Instead, feel yourself expanded in that space. Then exhale and inhale in this global feeling. There is no pushing in the exhalation, no grasping in the inhalation. Be aware of it. There is no end-gaining. On the next exhalation do not control any more. Let the breath have its natural flow. Try to keep the feeling of this expansion.

(pause)

Is there something which is not clear in your observation? One must be aware that, at first, one occupies only parts of the body in the exhalation and inhalation. So you must occupy the whole volume, lower, middle and upper parts. When there is agitation in your body, you will also feel it in the breathing. Through this breathing, using the whole torso, which is the natural way one breathes, you can make the mind tranquil. One could also say that the "I-image" is a contraction of the body. Feeling the expansion of your body in space eliminates the hold of the "I." When there is nervousness and agitation, when there is doubt, it is appropriate to do the breathing. Be careful to localize the breathing several inches in front of the nostrils; since the olfactory nerves are the nearest to our brain, if the breathing is not in front of the nostrils, it may strike the top of the nasal passage, and you may have a burning sensation or become dizzy or get a headache. You know, we live almost constantly in anticipation. But when you do this exercise here, you are completely one with the flow from moment to moment, with no anticipation to an end, or to a beginning.

Are there any questions?

When you asked us to feel the space behind, there was a moment when my mind started to question whether this is something I am genuinely feeling, or a fantasy.

There is no fantasy in it. It is really a tactile sensation. There is no mind, only perception.

It is not quite clear. Do you use the mind for a second to visualize the space behind?

Yes.

And then you let go of all the visualization and just go in with the tactile sensation?

Visualize your knee, the anatomy of your knee. You can visualize space in the knee, and when you visualize space in the knee, there is only vision, but not sensing. There is only the image. Then you go away from the vision and you feel how the vision has acted on your knee. You will feel the sensation of space in the knee. And your knee will move in a completely different way. There is no thinking in it. Merely sensation.

Do you remember when you were a little boy and you saw a big hole in front of you? What did you do? You did this. (*Dr. Klein stands up and sways backwards and forwards as if preparing to spring over a hole; then he jumps.*) Now what did you do here? First, you did it so-called mentally, but it is not with the mind, it is with the tactile feeling. The moment you jump with your tactile feeling, you are no longer here but already there. A dancer does not dance in one spot, the dancing is in the whole space. This feeling has nothing to do with the mind or with the imagination; it is not imagination.

Could one call it tactile visualization?

Yes. That is a very good expression. When you are rock-climbing in the mountains and you have a hold here and here, and you must put your foot somewhere, what do you do? Before actually doing it, you do it with the energy body. It is not imagination, it is real.

In the exercise we visualized the space in front, and then the space on the left and the space on the right. These three we can do together and separately, but then you asked us to visualize the space behind?

Yes, and you could no longer visualize in front at the same time.

Yes, I tried to do it and I saw that it can't be done, and the question is, why?

You can only visualize yourself, your body, in certain directions—in front, left, right, or behind. You can only see fractions, you can never visualize the whole. It is not possible. You cannot visualize it, but you can feel it.

Is this because the visualization uses one sense and the global feeling uses all of them?

Absolutely. You can visualize your front and then visualize your back, but you cannot visualize both together. But you can have a global feeling of both. What we call space, length and breadth appears to be a simultaneous perception, but that is not the case. In fact, we only see one of them at a time. The succession is very fast, and then we speak of a whole, but in reality we can never perceive this whole. There are three directions, but to realize the three directions you need a fourth direction. The fourth direction is time. To go from here to there takes time. So there is no space without time. Generally, in what we call space there is much memory. We complete it with our memory.

I would like to ask, please, about expansion. Is it that we feel an enlargement of the normal shape of the body and at the same time, as if there is an internal film of the body, we see the organs and the inner parts of the body? Is that what you mean by expansion, or have I not understood correctly?

In one way you have understood correctly. The organs of the body occupy a certain dimension, which we can feel and visualize in expansion. This is useful especially for healing. But the body is not limited to these measures. We have created boundaries to the body. We have fixed it to conform to what we can see. And because we identify with our body-mind, we have put ourselves into these boundaries. We have put ourselves into a cage. But if you close your eyes and free yourself from the accepted dimension of your hand, the feeling hand comes up. And you will see that your hand has completely other dimensions than the one you created with your eyesight.

There is an envelope around the body which is much wider than the eyesight has outlined. You can feel this expanded energy body when you are in a dark room and you spread yourself in all directions to get oriented and not hurt yourself. You are not here, you are already over there. The fact is that there is a kind of energy body beyond the physiological envelope. You will become conscious of this vital envelope. When you speak of expansion, you speak of this vital envelope, the transparent body, the radiant body. When we are sensitive to every new place, we automatically appropriate ourselves to the space. We go completely in the space, make it our own. When we make it our own, we are in the global. When we knowingly live the expansion, we live in our globality.

What is the use of this body?

Of the vital body? It is the real body. It is this vital body which prepares, helps, your physical body to be in a normal, healthy state.

Does this body die together with the physical body?

Yes. All that is perceived dies. The physical body is energy, and the vital body is finer energy. But the source is one energy. The life force, the power which has helped your body to grow, dissolves in this energy. All the localized energy which makes up a human body goes to the total

115

energy. Don't forget that this energy is lent to you temporarily.

To whom? To me?

For the pleasure to exist, and you exist only to inquire: Who am I?

Does the "I am," the feeling of being, also dissolve with the dissolution of the physical body?

The "I am" is. What you have been lent exists, and existence dies. Being is never born and never dies.

It seems to me that we are cut off from this light energy body.

It is not cut off, but this light body is paralyzed by our reactions.

Should we do these exercises when stillness invites us?

Yes. You will become more and more aware of a solicitation.

Does this becoming more aware of the solicitation come from doing the exercise, or will it come anyway?

It comes anyway. It comes when we no longer look for an end, when we know that there is no end, that the end is here and now. There is no beginning, no end. Only the now.

And when it happens, finally, that you live this feeling, do you feel that you are both outside and inside?

Do you mean your awareness?

Yes.

You are neither inside nor outside, you are nowhere. Awareness is nowhere. Awareness has no direction. Awareness is free from directions. You can never localize awareness.

Is this awareness part of being a human being and having a body?

Awareness is completely autonomous, dependent on nothing. It is in our awareness that what is perceived appears. All is perceived in awareness. But awareness is not in the perceived. If awareness were in the perceived, there could be no perceiving. It takes time to come to the deep comprehension that what is perceived needs a perceiver, that the subject that is in relation to an object is itself an object perceived, and that, in reality, all is in the perceiving. There is no autonomy of objects.

Please, what causes illness?

My first answer would be that it is a deep reaction. For example, suppose you have a very high opinion of yourself. Society has given you so many things, and the result is that you greatly value yourself in the society and your vitality, your strength as a male. You may be quite fixed in this image that society and your surroundings have made of you. That is your "I" position. Then, one day someone says, "You are a fool." And what happens? You may be very shocked, and you may have such a strong reaction that it acts on your liver, your spinal cord, your lungs, your spleen and so on. The reaction is psychological, but you feel its repercussions on the biological level. You might become white, or red. The reaction may affect some organs more than others. Not all our organs are equally strong. The reaction may strike the weak parts of the body, causing illness.

When an illness appears on the body level after a reaction, does visualizing the past help?

You can go back to the past occasionally, but first face the situation in its actuality, how it affects you now. Fifteen or twenty years ago you faced a situation from the personal point of view, you were psychologically involved in the situation, and this created the reaction. But if you now take a stance in your globality and emptiness of mind, from this position you can recreate the situation, visualize it and the feelings it caused in you at the time. You may find that just visualizing the situation causes the old feelings, the old reaction, to come up. But when it comes up in your impersonal globality, you no longer give a hold to it, and if you do this a few times, the old reaction will not come up.

Should you repeat this exercise as often as necessary until the old pattern no longer appears?

Yes.

You are talking about looking at a past situation. But if I can face it from the global view and emptiness of mind, I am already over the situation. How can one get over a situation that is still very raw, still causing a lot of feeling?

It is better to be accustomed to the non-objective approach when not in a crisis, then you may be able to face the crisis from this approach. Otherwise, you must sense your reaction as soon as you can, then face again the situation fron non-selection.

What about illness in children?

You must deal with a child as you deal with absolute perfection. A child is the absolute perfection.

Why do children have illnesses, then?

When you correct a child, you must do it with the background that the child comes from perfection and is perfection. And from perfection you go to what is not perfect. For example, you might say, "Look how well, how beautifully, you proceed, you do this, you do that, your reasoning is very good, your behavior is very good. But perhaps if you can transpose what you do so well here to here, it would be perfect." Then there is no reaction in the child. You must never say, "This is not good," or there will be a reaction. When you go from the positive to the negative, then the negative is seen completely differently.

Because there is no judgment?

Exactly. But you don't need all these details. When you love the child, you behave well.

You said that children are perfect. If so, why do they sometimes have car accidents or fall off a wall? I am afraid of this, because I have a small daughter.

But the life of a child is an adventure. It appropriates itself in space and time. And in this adventure there are risks. But still, the child comes from perfection.

I would like to ask, what is forgiveness?

When there is love, there is forgiveness. From the point of view of the person, there is never forgiving because then forgiving is only intellectual. In love there's not a forgiver. As long as there's a forgiver, there cannot be total forgiveness.

The artist feels a certain agony in trying to transfer what he feels into his work. How can he face this agony?

The artist feels deep joy. When he is gifted, he can express this joy through volumes, colors, or sounds. He may have an insight of the whole work, but when it comes to expressing, in space and time, the representation that he had in one moment, he may find it impossible to do it justice. The exteriorization of his vision is imperfect. Not having the possibility to express what one saw at a certain moment, perhaps in the state between sleeping and waking, or in a dream, or even before dropping off to sleep, brings one to a very deep sadness. The artist feels deeply sad that he cannot really express what he saw in this moment.

But the initial motive to create the thing in space and time has nothing to do with agony. It is to share with others deep joy. When you go very very deep, producing art is a way of thanking, thanking for being allowed to be.

Let us take a break for ten minutes.

In my everyday life I have a lot of duties. When I am here, I feel that I am not so involved in these duties, but I am afraid that when I go back I will get involved again. So the question is: What is duty?

Life has put you in a situation, and life asks you to execute the situation in which life put you. But there is no doer; don't take yourself for a doer. The most important thing for you when you go back home is that you look, not from the personal point of view, not from the psychological point of view, but look at your situation objectively as the scientist looks. If you do this, if you look at the facts as facts, you will see that there is no burden at all. Then there will be simply doing, acting, living, but no doer, no one who lives. If you are not psychologically involved in something, there is great joy in doing it, because you will discover in this so-called duty things that you never saw before. This duty will never be repetitious. It will be new at every moment, because you are free from all patterns. In doing without the doer, things flow harmoniously, spontaneously. But don't fall in the trap that, after doing, you say, "I did it." You can only say, "I can memorize what has been done; that means that I was witness to it." In doing, there is only doing. As we said yesterday, Mozart composed many operas, but at the moment of composing, Mozart was absent; Shakespeare wrote many dramas, but at the moment of writing, Shakespeare was not present. Napoleon won many wars, but at the moment of winning Napoleon was absent

You mean Napoleon had no ego involvement when he was making war? In the moment of the war I don't see how you can say there was no ego present!

There was acting. From where the acting springs is of no interest here. There is only acting.

Your example of Shakespeare is easier to understand than your example of Napoleon!

You are English, so you don't like Napoleon! (everyone laughs)

By the same token, could we say there was no Hitler, or murderer, or what have you?

In the moment of doing, there was only doing. This by no means excuses Hitler; whereas Mozart and Shakespeare were one with creative joy at the moment of composing, Hitler and Napoleon were identified with their self-images. The so-called actions of Hitler were only reactions. Being identified with the self-image and acting out of reaction is not exclusive to the great tyrants of history. It belongs to all of us. We are all an accomplice to the evil in the world, consciously or unconsciously.

In the moment itself there was no Napoleon, but later he said, "I did it." (laughter)

And for that they put him in prison! (laughter)

And we, too, say, "I did it," and put ourselves in prison. What can be done to get out of the prison?

When you see that you are in the prison, your seeing is from outside the prison. It is awareness, so be the awareness. The entity who longs for freedom belongs to the prison. The entity can never free the entity. When you see it, you are beyond the bars, so be the seeing. The moment this is clear to you, be the freedom knowingly, not intellectually. Be it with your totality.

When you don't take yourself for an independent entity, you spontaneously collaborate with life, and it is easy and there is joy in it. But the moment you take life personally, that is, you take yourself for somebody, you are psychologically involved and there is suffering. In reality, there is no one to be bound and no one to be free.

But the desire to be free comes from freedom itself? Does it not?

Yes. But the entity who desires comes from bondage. So follow your desire, free from the one who desires.

You said that when I see that trying to be out of the prison belongs to the prison, I should knowingly be the seeing. What is the bridge between seeing something and being the seeing?

When the seen dissolves in the seeing, the whole psychosomatic body is included. Feel how the seeing acts on you, how your psychosomatic body feels expanded. Abide in this feeling. Let it unfold.

(pause)

During our being together we spent moments in the joy of being free from objects. These moments of objectless joy are seeds in us which are waiting to grow. When you go home you will sometimes be solicited by these moments, even in the middle of your daily activities. You do not need to make an effort to remember these unconditioned moments or these sayings, because joy looks for itself. Live only in alertness, as you have here. Abide in welcoming, in availability to the present moment, free from anticipation and end-gaining. It is in being available and listening in openness to our surroundings that beauty, understanding and right action appear. Be in identity with these moments when they come to you.

It was a great joy to be with you, to be one with you in the land of Plato and Socrates. In this joy, this oneness, there is no separation.

For further information regarding Jean Klein and his schedule of talks and seminars in the United States and Eurore, write to the Jean Klein Foundation, P.O. Box 940, Larkspur, CA 94977.

Those interested in Jean Klein's teachings may also wish to subscribe to the journal *LISTENING*, published twice a year. For subscription rates, write to the Jean Klein Foundation, P.O. Box 2111, Santa Barbara, CA 93120.